12

KENT

&

THE BATTLE OF BRITAIN

The Long Hot Summer of 1940

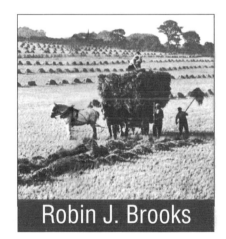

Robin J. Brooks

COUNTRYSIDE BOOKS
3 Catherine Road
Newbury, Berkshire

To view our complete range of books,
please visit us at
www.countrysidebooks.co.uk

ISBN 978 1 84674 165 4

Designed by Peter Davies, Nautilus Design
Produced through MRM Associates Ltd., Reading
Printed by Information Press, Oxford

*All material for the manufacture of this book
was sourced from sustainable forests.*

Contents

INTRODUCTION

In **July 1940** the German Luftwaffe was committed by its Commander-in-chief, Reichmarshall Hermann Goering, to destroying the RAF. Victories in Poland, Denmark, Norway, Holland, Belgium and France had convinced him that he would have command of the skies above Britain in one week. That this never happened was due mainly to Fighter Command, tasked with the defence of the country, and the British determination inspired by the Prime Minister, Winston Churchill. The brunt of the fighting was to be in the area controlled by 11 Group, Fighter Command. This encompassed the south-east corner of England, including Kent. For four months the whole fury of the Luftwaffe was directed against this county, earning it the dubious title of 'Hell Fire Corner'.

From the beginning, tales of heroism became news. They not only told of individual acts by pilots and ground crews of the RAF or of the Army, but also the civilian services. Much has been written and recorded in detail about the aerial struggle against a numerically superior air force. This is not the familiar day-to-day account of the battle but one that records the human story, woven from the little-recorded first-hand accounts of the summer of 1940. It is not possible to record every incident and for this, I apologize, but I hope that this book will give the reader a flavour of those desperate times. I therefore dedicate the following pages to all those services and civilians involved, those who died in the struggle, those who were injured and those left behind.

Robin J. Brooks

Acknowledgements

I acknowledge with grateful thanks all the individuals and organisations who have assisted me in the writing of this book. I list them in no particular order:

Ronald F Blay - Brian Hussey - Monty Banks - Alan Major FBNA - Mr N. Bentley - David Leslie Taylor - Mrs Pat Philpott - Leslie Pearce - Winston Ramsey - *After the Battle magazine* - Springfield Library, Maidstone - Lashenden Air Warfare Museum.

My appreciation also to Tony Webb of Maidstone for allowing me to include material in Chapter 6 from his publication *Battle Over Kent*, first published in 1977.

Thanks go, too, to my wife Barbara who has suffered my long absences and also for her proof reading skills.

A special note of gratitude goes to the *Kent Messenger* newspaper and in particular to Barry Hollis, their picture manager for the use of many of the KM pictures.

Chapter 1

Getting Ready to Fight the Enemy

It was thanks to Prime Minister Neville Chamberlain's 'peace in our time' appeasement of Hitler in 1938 and, later, to the quiet period after the declaration of war in September 1939, known as the 'phoney war', that England was allowed hurriedly to test and practise the methods by which we would defend ourselves against the Luftwaffe and German plans for invasion.

No. 11 Group Fighter Command, controlling the south-east corner of the country, was given time to strengthen and further prepare the squadrons that would fly from the Kent airfields. The early warning radar stations along the coast and inland at Dunkirk near Canterbury, known as 'Chain Home' stations, were able to carry out further exercises, allowing the operators of the equipment to become even more proficient. Along with the Observer Corps, they were to become our first line of defence against the Luftwaffe.

As the crisis deepened in August 1939, the civilian authorities in Kent were also coming together to fight the enemy. Gas masks were being issued lest a gas attack took place as it had on the Western Front during the First World War. Black cloth began to rapidly sell out as people were told to cover every window in their houses at night. The slightest chink of light showing was considered to be an open invitation to enemy aircraft and an even greater danger if and when an invasion came.

And of that time, there was no doubt! The rapid thrust of the German military machine across the Low Countries in the late summer of 1939 gave every indication

Wry humour from a Maidstone driver who was determined that his family's holiday would not be spoilt by the Germans.

that it would not stop at the French Channel coast. Preparations were therefore put in hand to evacuate mothers and children, pregnant women and some schoolteachers from Kent to safer parts of the country. The exercise was code-named 'Operation Pied Piper'. Each little evacuee carried a small suitcase or paper parcel containing a few clothes and some food. With gas mask holders hanging from their shoulders and a brown label attached to their outer garment giving their name, age and religion, many tearful scenes were played out at railway stations in Kent and across the country. The statistics were staggering. On the move in September 1939 were 827,000 school children, 524,000 pre-school children and their mums, 12,000 pregnant mothers and 103,000 teachers and helpers. It was the biggest domestic migration ever.

Strangely however, the first wave of evacuation did not last long. The expected

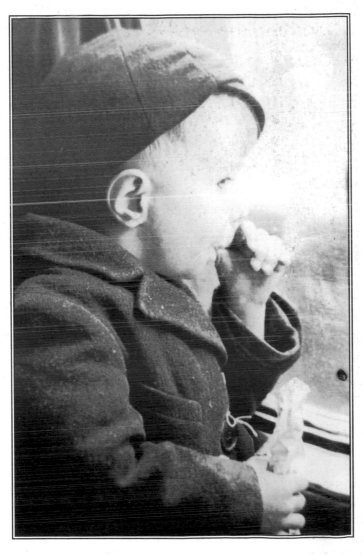

A 'Pied Piper' evacuee.

invasion did not happen and by Christmas 1939 three out of four children had returned home. There was a second wave in 1940 and a final phase in the summer of 1944. In addition, more than 70,000 children were evacuated abroad. One lasting important debate that 'Pied Piper' is assumed to have instigated, however, was to highlight the gulf between the social classes. It appears to have played a hand in the wish to create a fairer society for the future.

As a four-year-old, Brian Coy of Gravesend was one of the 'Pied Piper' infants:

> We were evacuated on Sunday, 3rd September 1939. Early in the morning we were processed and issued labels and taken down to the river and put aboard one of the Thames pleasure steamers, *The Golden Eagle*. We steamed down the Thames and as we came into the North Sea it was announced that war had officially been declared.
>
> The ship had orders to be converted to a minesweeper after it had dropped us off, so the crew started giving away all the cakes and sweets on board. When we hit the open sea we were a bunch of sea-sick kids. We were heading for Great Yarmouth in Norfolk and when we arrived at the docks, for temporary housing they put us in the stables at Yarmouth race track. We were given piles of clean sacks and hay and told to settle down for the night. The next day we were given carrier bags full of food, tinned milk, corned beef, tinned fruit and chocolate bars and put on coaches to go to our final billets. We ended up on a farm where, among other things, they raised thoroughbred greyhounds and dalmations. They fed the dogs better than they fed us. Mum, who was pregnant with twins, lost one of the babies.
>
> It was not very nice and after six weeks mum brought us home. We stayed in Gravesend until the V2s started coming and I was evacuated again but this time to Cumberland.

Brian was one of the many millions of children who left their homes in 1939 and this was just one of the preparations that had to be made as war became imminent. For months beforehand, the government and the civilian authorities had taken the threat of air raids seriously. Gas was thought to be one of the major dangers, with the first measures in anti-gas training being taken at the Corn Exchange in Maidstone as early as March 1936. It was here that 60 men and women, members of the St John Ambulance, gathered for an intensive training schedule. Once qualified, it was their duty to train a vast number of civilians in similar procedures.

Government ministers came to the county to talk about government policy

Saying goodbye.

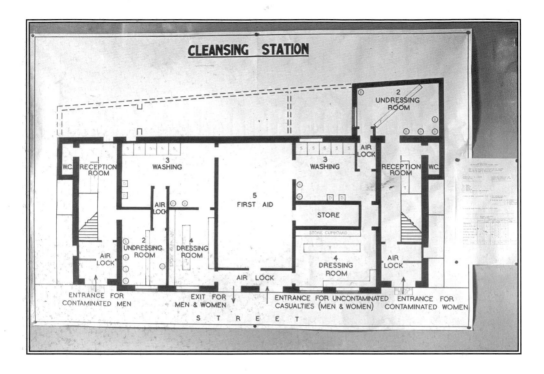

One of the many cleansing stations in Kent. This one was set up in
St George's Hotel, Deal. (Kent Messenger -ref. PD1537062)

relating to air-raid precautions. Mr Geoffrey Lloyd, the Under-Secretary of State to the Home Office, visited Ashford Corn Exchange in March 1938. His speech applauded the fact that many Kent authorities had done very well in recruiting civilians to such bodies as the Air Raid Precautions (ARP) and the emergency services. However, many more were needed in this hour of need if the country was not to fall. His words did not go unheeded as both men and women, who for some reason could not volunteer for active service, rose to the occasion and joined the civilian services.

At the same time, the RAF in Kent was establishing itself on the airfields. To Biggin Hill was to fall the role of a sector or controlling station. The airfield had been an experimental site in air-to-ground wireless telephony and instrument design since the armistice following the First World War in 1918. Over the intervening years it had been extended and a vast programme of reconstruction had taken place.

In May 1936 the Home Defence Force was reorganised into four functional commands: Bomber, Fighter, Coastal and Training. Biggin Hill, known affectionately

Getting Ready to Fight the Enemy

*The eagle of the RAF is seen as a breakwater
from Folkestone cliffs. (Author)*

as 'Biggin on the Bump' (due to its location on the top of the North Downs), was to be first and foremost a fighter station in charge of Sectors 'C' and 'D'. Other stations in the sectors were Gravesend, Lympne, West Malling, Hawkinge, Manston and the Coastal Command airfields of Detling and Eastchurch. Of these, Manston, Gravesend, Lympne and Hawkinge were known as 'forward airfields', where detached units from the main airfields could re-arm and refuel in order to be at a 'state of advanced readiness'. Only one airfield in Sector C was not finished at the outbreak of war. Throughout the Battle of Britain, West Malling was under construction although it was used in emergencies. Not until the end of the Battle, deemed to be October 1940, did it become fully operational.

During the 1930s some of these airfields had looked neat and pristine, with gardens faithfully tended, buildings painted brightly and kerbstones painted white. The Empire Air Days of the period had attracted the public in their thousands, all eager to see the RAF at work and to admire the care lavished upon the airfields. With the threat of war, however, the brightly-painted buildings were hastily camouflaged

Getting Ready to Fight the Enemy

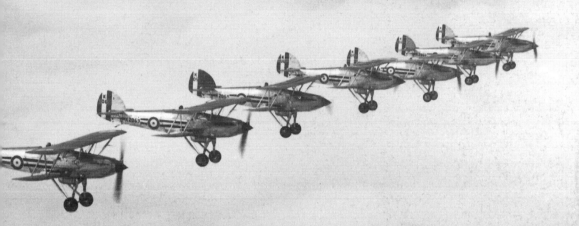

The halcyon days of flying in 1938-39. No 25 Squadron show off their formation expertise in their Hawker Furies whilst flying from Hawkinge. (Flight)

to avoid making them obvious from the air. The roofs of hangars and other large buildings were subject to thousands of gallons of paint. Landing areas were made to look like 'farmers' fields' by painting parallel lines to represent hedgerows. Various types of pill boxes were placed around each airfield, with air-raid shelters being hastily dug in case the airfields came under heavy bomb attack. All of these preparations were none too soon as September 1939 approached and the news from Europe made grim reading.

On Friday, 1st September of that year, Germany invaded Poland. Shortly before 6 am German forces crossed the Polish border after a period of heavy aerial bombardment. It soon became obvious that nothing could stop the German war machine until it reached the Channel coast. Even then it appeared as though it might achieve what Napoleon never did – crossing the English Channel. That the invasion never happened was down to a number of factors and the bravery of the many. However, before we come to those fateful four months known as the Battle of Britain, we must look back at the last few months of 1939.

The station band at Detling, 1934-40.

Chapter 2

On a War Footing

The Winter of 1939-40

f the summer of 1940 was to prove one of the hottest on record, then the winter of 1939-40 was one of the coldest. When war broke out on 3rd September 1939, it heralded a period of frost and snow not usually seen so early in the winter. At Detling airfield, perched high on the North Downs, near Maidstone, the first members of the Women's Auxiliary Air Force (WAAF) had arrived. Among them was Maidstone girl, Ann Tebbutt. A member of the 19th Company (County of Kent) WAAF, she was now to be on active service.

Ann had become interested in joining up at about the time of the Munich crisis in 1938. She walked into the local army recruiting office in Maidstone and to the horror of the recruiting sergeant, announced that she would prefer to join the air force. 'You want the other end of the town for that lot,' choked the sergeant. Dutifully Ann went to 57 London Road, which was the recruiting centre for the RAF, and enlisted in the 19th Company, an offspring of the Royal West Kent Regiment. She received her number, 882009, and was told to await a letter confirming her appointment in the unit.

After a period of time she joined the other 24 girls that were to make up the nucleus of the WAAF establishment attached to No 500 (County of Kent) Squadron of the Auxiliary Air Force. Recalling the initial training, it was found to be less than glamorous:

> We used to attend one anti-gas lecture every week at our headquarters at
> Astley House in Maidstone. We used to wonder just what the men thought

Bristol Blenheims of No 601 Squadron, Biggin Hill, September 1939. (RAF Museum)

when they saw us coming into the room. I remember how hideous we all looked in those dreadful masks, not at all becoming! However, I think the final straw for the men came when our WAAF officer told us we were so good at drill that Flt Sgt Smart of the RAF intended to put us on the square to show the men just how it was to be done.

When we were mobilised we did not have any trades as such. When the officer in charge asked us what we wanted to do, I was so keen that I just wanted to shout, 'Oh, I'll be a cook!' Thank goodness I did not when later on that day I saw just what a cook had to do in very primitive conditions.

The living quarters for this 25-strong band of girls were situated in some cottages on the edge of the airfield. Known as Binbury Cottages, they had no heating save a small coal fire which gave out minimal warmth. The girls froze and the wind and snow seemed to creep in everywhere. Perhaps Ann had the best idea:

My father drove up Detling Hill with my eiderdown and a hot water bottle from home. The water tower on the camp froze which entailed filling a kettle with snow to get enough hot water for my bottle. The same water went back and forth until the thaw came. Even the Air Ministry noticed the cold and orders were sent down that every girl was to be issued with an airman's overcoat.

At Biggin Hill, Nos 32 and 79 Squadrons were already in residence. Still equipped with Gloster Gauntlets, the pilots could only look on enviously as a Hawker Hurricane flew in, the first to be seen close up by most of the pilots and ground crews. However, this was the first of the many, for the Hurricane was to become the symbol of aerial fighting over the next few summer months. Only later was the Supermarine Spitfire to join in the eventual defeat of the Luftwaffe.

By 1939 the civil defence organisations in the Kentish towns and the defences on the ground were already on a war footing. So eager were the latter that on Wednesday, 6th September, a radar station along the coast plotted a force of aircraft, thought to be enemy, heading towards the Thames estuary. The information was passed on to the Fighter Command filter room at Stanmore in Middlesex who alerted the sector stations in the Home Counties. At 6.50 am the force was plotted well up the estuary and the order was sent out to scramble several aircraft. The

Detling WAAFs have fun in the heavy snowfalls of 1939-40. (RAF Detling)

'My appearance caused hoots of laughter, wolf whistles, and good natured, if somewhat uncomplimentary advice,' wrote Mary Twyman, one of over 4,000 Land Army girls, seen here at Mote Park, Maidstone, during a rally.

air raid sirens began to wail for the third time since war was declared and the anti-aircraft gunners on the ground trained their guns on the sky above.

Rather too late it was realised that the 'attacking' force was a flight consisting of twin-engined Bristol Blenheims. Sadly, the incident became the first case of 'friendly fire' in the war when one Blenheim was shot down by the ground gunners and two of the Hurricanes sent up to intercept were also shot down, with one of the pilots being killed. Later, the reason given for the radar reporting error was that the 'Chain Home' radar station had developed a technical fault which gave a false reading. This tragic incident so early in the war became known as the 'Battle of Barking Creek'.

These opening phases were a testing time. Itchy fingers were constantly on the trigger and every aircraft that entered our air space was thought to be hostile. The ARP book, or 'War Book' as it is now called, in the Maidstone archives, records another case of mistaken reporting:

> At 11.30 pm a local searchlight crew reported hearing aircraft engines overhead. No other units in the surrounding area had picked up any sounds nor had any radar reports been filed. Still the searchlight crew insisted the sound detection system had picked up aircraft engines. Coming to full alert and having informed Biggin Hill who sent up a fighter (though just what a day fighter could do at night is debatable) to investigate, it was suddenly realised that someone had left the refrigerator door open in the mess hut and the sensitive sound locating equipment had picked up the sounds of the motor.

On Monday, 4th September, His Majesty the King broadcast a message to the Empire: 'In this grave hour, perhaps the most fateful in our history, I send to every household of my people, both at home and overseas, this message, spoken with the same depth of feeling for each one of you as if I were able to cross your threshold and speak to you myself. For the second time in the lives of most of us we are at war. Over and over again we have tried to find a peaceful way out of the differences between ourselves and those who are now our enemies.'

He went on to finish: 'If one and all we keep resolutely faithful to it, ready for whatever service or sacrifice it may demand, then, with God's help, we shall prevail. May he bless and keep us all.'

The *Daily Sketch* newspaper dated that day printed the King's message in full. The following pages gave details of the military men who would lead the war effort, together with a headline stating that Winston Churchill was back at the Admiralty as

'*All right then – loser pays for a Spitfire.*'
A topical cartoon from a 1940 edition of Punch *magazine.*

A poster of the 1939-40 period.

First Sea Lord. An article by Lady Oxford outlined what the country would be fighting for. She called it a 'miracle crusade' in which all right-thinking men were protected by the same armour, united by the same convictions and fighting under the same banner.

That the latter was true could not be disputed as many hundreds of Polish airmen arrived at the Coastal Command base at Eastchurch on the Isle of Sheppey. Devoid of aircraft at the time, this was now the Polish Training Centre for all those bewildered Poles who had fled their own country when it was invaded and wished to carry on the fight from British soil. The cruel winter of 1939-40 did not have the same effect on them as their British counterparts for they were hardened to the frost and snow in Poland. By March 1940, 1,300 Polish airmen were billeted at Eastchurch, taking lessons in English and getting to know the

Polish airmen learning the 'English' way, Eastchurch 1940.

layouts of various British aircraft. This was also the first introduction for the majority to the 'fair sex', as many menial tasks such as cooking for the Polish airmen were given over to local women.

Eager to play their part, thousands of women found themselves trying to hold down a full-time job whilst managing their homes. In line with government policy, women were not allowed to do 'front line' duties but could join such organisations as the Women's Voluntary Service and Civil Defence. Whilst many did, others chose to work in munitions factories such as Tilling-Stevens in Maidstone. Here they produced various armaments including shells, all of it very dangerous work involving explosives. The Women's Land Army was set up in June 1939 to work the land whilst many of the male farm workers were away on active service. At its peak,

Women were encouraged to take up factory work.

A women's warden post in Rochester. (Kent Messenger -ref. PD1447878)

Woman fire guard using a stirrup pump. (Poppofoto)

80,000 land girls dressed in their traditional green sweater, brown breeches, brown felt hat and khaki overcoat were carrying out hard labour in the fields. In this hour of need, the nation still had to be fed.

Everywhere there were signs of preparation for war. Even the hospitals were getting a coat of camouflage paint to deny the enemy bombers a target. The late Cyril Turner of Canterbury was doing just that when war was declared that very morning:

> Working at the Kent and Canterbury Hospital, our final job was to hide the two white paths leading to the hospital and Sunday was the best day for that. At 11 o'clock the sirens began to wail and, after a few anxious nervous looks at the sky, we carried on painting the path and various other buildings. Alas, speeding towards us on her bicycle came a lady ARP warden blowing furiously on her whistle. She ordered us into a ditch nearby, with instructions

Wardens erecting barbed wire along the Kent coast at Margate.
(Kent Messenger -ref.PD1466000)

to stay there. We had a smoke and with nothing happening in the sky above, got out and carried on again. But once again the lady appeared with her whistle and we had to explain to her the urgency of our work. With that she seemed satisfied and went away. By 2 pm we were home eating our dinners and pleased we had got the job done in time.

In Deal, the late Bill Pitchford, who owned a confectionery and greengrocer's shop, was busy with his own preparations for war:

We all listened to the speech by Mr Chamberlain and the men who lived close to the rear of my shop had a quick meeting and decided to start to dig a trench at the bottom of my neighbour's garden. The entrance was to be on a small piece of land at the back of the shop. Digging started at once and I took my hand cart up to the Yew Tree Hotel where there was a dog track that I knew had closed and which was selling off building materials. I managed to get some new corrugated sheets, 6 ft by 2 ft, selling at ten for £1. I came back with 20 sheets and we used these to cover the shelter. Earth from the trench went on top. We eventually had everything in except the kitchen sink! This shelter we used until the government built a concrete shelter on a spare piece of ground. Had a bomb dropped even nearby, I often wonder if we would have survived in our home-built shelter.

Back at Detling airfield, No 500 (County of Kent) Auxiliary Squadron was busy converting from its aged Hawker Hind biplanes to the more modern twin-engine Avro Anson. I use the term 'modern' very loosely for, even by 1939, the aircraft was obsolete and certainly no match for the numerically superior Luftwaffe. As part of No 16 (General Reconnaissance) Group of Coastal Command, the role of the squadron was reconnaissance over the Channel and Dover Straits, together with convoy escort duties. The Anson was armed with just two .303 guns firing forward and another in a turret aft of the cabin, so the Commanding Officer, Sqd Ldr LeMay, ordered two additional machine guns to be fitted to fire through the side windows. In addition, an enormous 20 mm cannon was fitted to his own aircraft to fire through the bottom of the fuselage. With the gun mounting designed and manufactured by the aforementioned Tilling-Stevens of Maidstone, it was reckoned that when the cannon was fired, the Anson gained another 100 ft in height!

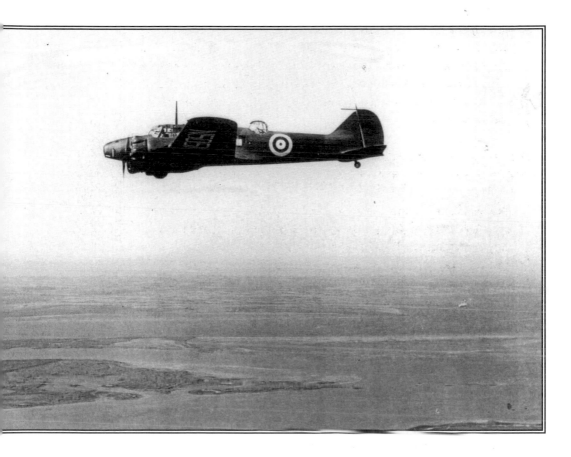

An Anson of No 500 Squadron on patrol. (R. Young)

With typical British idiosyncracy, the cold winter of 1939-40 brought forth many ideas to further the comfort of both troops and civilians. Many of them came from women. In a letter to *The Times* on 16th November 1939, showing the spirit in the country at this time, Miss Ethel Purcell of Blackheath wrote:

> Sir,
> You were good enough to insert a letter from me appealing for old gloves to be made into wind-proof waistcoats. I write now to thank you and to tell you that the response has surpassed my expectations. I have already received over 500 pairs of gloves, several old golfing and leather coats, and some parcels of cuttings from leather-work, all most useful for my purpose. My friends and I hope to make many waistcoats as a result.

The long period known as the 'phoney war' was ebbing to its close and, as 1940 dawned, so came a period known as the 'twilight war'. The New Year would see the full onslaught of the enemy, leading to what Hitler and the German High Command hoped would be the invasion of the British Isles. When and if it came, Kent, the closest county to the Continent, would be in the front line.

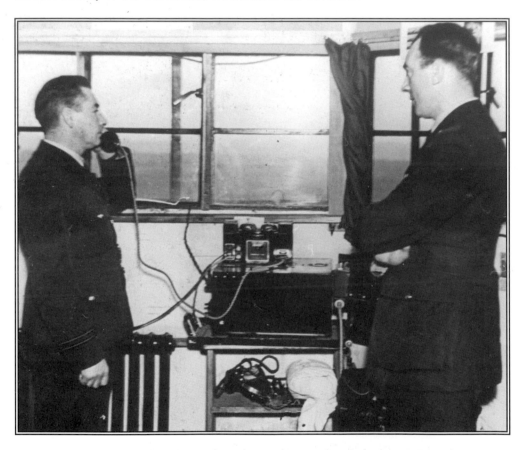

Fl/Lt E. Rossington and Sqd Ldr Ward in Gravesend control tower.
(Kent Messenger -ref. PD1560152)

Chapter 3

Rescue from Dunkirk

January to June 1940

January 1940 saw the county a little further prepared for war. Any thoughts of, 'Oh, it will all be over by Christmas' had quickly evaporated as the German military machine overran country after country. The months of January, February and March were to become a period of hectic and intense preparation for what everyone feared would happen.

Seeing the carnage on the Continent, the government and the local authorities stockpiled air raid shelters to be issued or sold to the public. The most common was the Anderson shelter, a semi-sunk structure consisting of a curved steel roof, supported by stronger and thicker steel girders. Named after the then Home Secretary, Sir John Anderson and designed by a Scottish engineer, William Patterson, it was provided free to manual workers in danger areas and to any family with an income under £250 a year. Over that income you purchased one for £7!

For people living along the Kent coast, the cliffs provided an adequate shelter against bombs, as Dick Whittamore remembers:

> In the cliffs beneath Dover, there were many caves from days gone by. They were opened for wartime use in addition to the other type of shelters on offer. They were very damp, being chalk and were not very warm. There were several in the town, especially in the seafront areas, including one beneath Woolworths. There were other basement shelters in the town with

A wartime shelter dug into the bank at Folkestone. (Author)

signs directing you to them. Air raid warnings were tested before the war to get people used to them but when they sounded because a raid was imminent, people thought they were just testing them and were in no rush to get into a shelter.

Another type that came into use was the Morrison shelter. This is best described as a steel cage that was erected within the confines of the house, usually the kitchen or lounge, and served both as a table to eat from and also a cage in which to sleep. The strong steel top was said to be able to withstand any bomb that hit the house.

All of this preparation for war, however, seemed great fun to young children. Alan Major, of Canterbury, a Fellow of the British National Academy, was one of them:

> In July 1940 I left the council school for infants and moved at the end of August to Rainham Senior School in Orchard Street. A large part of each

Glum faces as an Anderson shelter is erected during 1939. (Kent Messenger)

end of the school was sandbagged and also used by the ARP. South of Rainham on open high ground near Park Wood was an anti-aircraft gun site with several guns. The searchlights were across country at Jack Clark's farm, Merescourt. There were some shelters but most of us, when the siren went, crowded into the class cloakrooms. I remember standing in there during one daylight raid when the guns were firing and the school windows rattled in their frames whilst the walls shook. However, when we got home in the evenings we used to go out and look for pieces of bomb casing or bullet cases. I had boxes of them, even a door off the bomber that crashed at Gore Bank, Upchurch.

As you may know, the long hot summer was preceded by the long cold winter. My father worked all his working life at Rainham Co-op as a shop assistant and grocery/bread delivery man. He had dreadful trouble getting around during the heavy snow. He was also in the ARP so when he got home he was straight back out again to make sure the blackout was observed and to assist if any bombs fell.

A crashed Anson at Detling with bombs aboard. (No 500 Squadron)

FO Dennis Maby, No 500 Squadron in his Avro Anson, Detling 1939.
He was killed 7th October 1939.

Back at Detling airfield, No 500 Squadron was carrying out Channel patrols, either escorting convoys through the Dover Strait or looking for stray mines in the shipping lanes. Already tragedy had struck the squadron with several Anson aircraft, together with their crews, being lost. One of the main factors was the appalling weather. Being high up on the North Downs, Detling was often subject to fog and difficult to find for returning aircraft. With no real blind-flying aids at this time, aircraft low on fuel would just have to come down wherever they could.

This invariably meant a crash landing, as in the case of Anson N5233 MK-Q. Having escorted Convoy OA16 from the North Foreland, the aircraft was returning to Detling in the dark when it suffered an engine failure. Although the aircraft was capable of flying on one engine for a limited time, on this occasion the weather was at its worst and did not help the situation. The pilot, Flying Officer D.G. Maby, ordered his crew, Pilot Officer A. Patterson, Corporal Drew and Leading Aircraftsman Messent,

Winston Churchill inspects a Home Guard platoon.

to bale out whilst he attempted what he hoped would be a safe crash landing near Benenden. The first to leave the aircraft was LAC Messent, who unfortunately clipped the tail of the aircraft as he jumped, rendering the aircraft unmanageable. The Anson plunged to the ground, killing the other three crew members. This was just one of several similar incidents to befall No 500 Squadron.

The Phoney War came to an end on 9th April when Germany invaded Denmark and Norway. As though this fact was recognised, the first bombs fell on Kent the next day, at Petham and Chilham, near Canterbury. With the threat of an invasion coming ever closer, Anthony Eden, the new Secretary of State for War, broadcast a radio appeal on 14th May for men not on active service to join a new home defence force called the 'Local Defence Volunteers'. Men between the ages of 17 and 65 were asked to come forward and sign on. Within 24 hours of Eden's speech, countrywide, a quarter of a million men had enrolled. At first the only uniform was an arm band proudly displaying the letters 'LDV'. By August the name had been changed to the 'Home Guard' and its integration with the local army regiments began.

A khaki uniform was issued but the armoury remained predominantly ancient with old First World War rifles, golf clubs, pick axe handles and even 'pepper' with which to attack an army (the latter was to weaken the vision of the enemy soldiers). The preferred weapon, however, was the 'Molotov Cocktail', a lethal combination of petrol in a glass bottle with an oily rag pushed into the neck. Once set alight, the idea was to throw it as far away as quickly as possible lest the entire bomb exploded in one's hand. It was known to be as dangerous to the carrier as it was to the recipient! It was felt by all, however, that if an invasion did take place, the Home Guard would fight alongside the rest of the military resources with zest.

During the last months of peace, arrangements had been made to send what was called a British Expeditionary Force (BEF) to France in an effort to help the French army stem the rapid advances of the German war machine. With them were to go four squadrons of Fighter Command aircraft, which left Britain five days after the war was declared. What has become known as the 'Battle of France' became a training ground in aerial combat for both the pilots and the ground crews. Yet despite this, at dawn on 10th May 1940, Hitler invaded the Low Countries with unimaginable speed, pushing the men and armour of the BEF to the coastal French town of Dunkirk.

Unbeknown at the time, a miracle was about to begin and for one soldier, Leslie Page, the period was to remain an indelible memory:

> We were told to make for Dunkirk, the only port in Allied hands. The Luftwaffe
> had bombed the oil tanks surrounding the port and the raging fires provided
> a constant landmark for us. Shelling started and our vehicles were parked

all around. We got into them and drove along the road heading away from the shelling. I remember our Colonel standing on the crossroads waving us all up the road away from the crossroads because the Jerry tanks were coming that way. We got out quickly and I remember jumping into a hedge of stinging nettles, with the shells dropping all around us, thinking that this was real war. As we came to the towns which were being bombed, the roads were full of refugees and we came to understand that this was a general retreat. Carriages were being pulled by horses which broke free when the planes were shelling and then the Luftwaffe started straffing the roads so we scattered across the fields. I asked someone where we were going. His reply was, 'Well, you see that smoke in the sky, that's Dunkirk. Make for that.'

Leslie Page, a soldier in the 44th Division of the Royal Army Ordnance Corps, did just that and was lucky to find a destroyer just leaving.

At Biggin Hill and at Gravesend, another pre-war civilian airfield requisitioned by the military, the fighter squadrons prepared to give cover to the beleaguered troops waiting to be rescued from the beaches. At 6.57 pm on 26th May, Vice Admiral

Deserted British lorries at Dunkirk.

Operation Dynamo – the Dunkirk operation.

Ramsey initiated *Operation Dynamo*, the evacuation of the BEF from France. A call went out for every available boat, whether large or small, to report to Dover, Folkestone or Ramsgate. Ferries, paddle steamers, tugs, barges, lifeboats and pleasure boats answered the call to cross the Channel and rescue the troops at Dunkirk. Eventually more than 700 brave little craft were cutting through the smooth sea.

As they set sail, Nos 32 and 79 Squadrons at Biggin Hill were sent away for a well earned rest. They had been in constant battle over the Channel since September 1939. In their place came No 610 (County of Chester) Auxiliary Squadron with Spitfires. They moved over to the satellite airfield at Gravesend whilst three Hurricane squadrons, Nos 229, 213 and 242 (Canadian), flew into Biggin Hill.

The day after their arrival, all the squadrons were in action over France. Down below, the pilots could see the little ships taking on troops, whilst their job was to keep the Luftwaffe at bay to allow the evacuation to continue. Such was the distance covered by the Hurricanes and Spitfires that they could only patrol for 40 minutes before low fuel forced them to turn back to base. Consequently, there were times when there was no air cover over the beaches and the question of 'Where is the RAF?' was often asked. Air Chief Marshal Keith Park, the Air Officer Commanding 11 Group, with just 16 squadrons at his disposal, was hard pressed to give constant cover during the daylight hours.

There were, however, other battles being fought in the air out of sight of the

Air Chief Marshal Sir Keith Rodney Park, Commander of
No 11 Group Fighter Command. (IWM)

beaches. Colin Gray from New Zealand was a 25-year-old pilot with No 54 Squadron. His baptism of fire came during the Dunkirk evacuation as retold in the book, *Battle of Britain Jubilee History* by Hough and Richards:

> Operation Dynamo started on 26th/27th May and was called off nine days later on June 4th. Fighter Command's involvement had actually begun ten days earlier when Hurricane and Spitfire squadrons of 11 Group started to fly patrols over the battle area. I am well aware of criticism aimed by members of the BEF and the Navy at the effectiveness, if not actual presence, of the RAF during this critical engagement. Well, we were there, anyway.
>
> My log book records a total of over 30 flying hours in the Calais/Boulogne/ Dunkirk area during the twelve days prior to our withdrawal from the front line on 28th May. We were flying two or three sorties a day with an average duration of two hours. Furthermore, our hours of readiness covered a period from dawn (say 4 am) to dusk at 10 pm. It was very tiring. Dunkirk was altogether a pretty torrid time for us. My most vivid recollection which I recall with no pride whatsoever, occurred on 25th May when we escorted a squadron of Swordfish aircraft to dive-bomb Gravelines. Their bombing was fairly ineffectual but they certainly managed to stir up a hornet's nest. In the subsequent mêlée, a German fighter placed a couple of cannon shells and numerous bullets into my aircraft. It served me right as I was watching a Me109 pilot bale out at the time. The first cannon shell went through the aft starboard inspection hatch, where it exploded, severing the elevator trimmers and knocking out the hydraulics and the air pressure system. The second shell passed over the top of the cockpit and through the port aileron, neatly removing the pitot head. My subsequent landing was not without its moments. The undercarriage came down with the aid of the emergency CO_2 bottle but the loss of air pressure meant no flaps or brakes and, with the pitot head shot away, no airspeed indicator. It was an interesting landing.

So ill-equipped were we that obsolete aircraft were brought in for front line duties. Pilot Officer D.H.Clarke reported for duty to Detling, flying a target-towing Blackburn Skua of No 2 Anti-aircraft Co-operation unit stationed at Gosport. His orders were to patrol each night west of Dunkirk, dropping powerful flares to light up any attempt by the German navy to interfere with the evacuation. Next morning, as his operation was not timed until after nightfall, he assisted ground crews who were working on about 50 Fleet Air Arm Fairey Swordfish aircraft which were due to take off on a fighter patrol across the beaches (the Swordfish was a torpedo-carrying aircraft). The idea was that the Germans would think the Swordfish to be the equally obsolescent Gladiator fighter and be frightened off by them.

The second patrol of the morning was flown by additional aircraft, including 37 Skuas and Blackburn Rocs. PO Clarke watched the return of a patrol just before lunchtime. It was not a pretty sight as described in my book *Kent's Own*:

> There were not many of the little aircraft left, I counted six. One of them belly-flopped on the grass and I went across to see what had happened. The aircraft was a complete write-off. Bullets and cannon shells had ripped the fuselage from end to end, the after cockpit was sprayed with blood. The front cockpit was worse. Two bullet holes through the back of the pilot's seat showed where he had been hit and his parachute, still in position, was saturated in blood. The instrument panel was shattered, and on the floor were the remains of a foot. I was physically sick where I stood at this sight.

Of the original force, nine aircraft came back and five were written off as they landed. The remaining four aircraft were airborne again within the hour. PO Clarke watched them go, 'They looked very pathetic limping back to Dunkirk all alone.'

Hawkinge – No 32 Squadron Hurricane P3522 about to scramble. (Fox Photos)

Dunkirk – troops disembarking at Admiralty Pier, Dover. They hand in their rifles before boarding the train. (via D. Collyer)

Safe and on their way home from Dunkirk to Dover.

Day after day, the struggle continued. No 610 Squadron managed eight kills and four probables but they lost six Spitfires, half the squadron. Up against overwhelming odds, the airmen fought valiantly, whilst from bases in Holland and France the Luftwaffe came in force in an attempt to thwart the evacuation. Each day 11 Group flew over 300 sorties, most leading to major combats.

On 1st June, the enemy had its biggest success when, in a bombing attack by Ju 87 Stukas, three destroyers and two large transport boats were sunk, with a heavy loss of life. Further tragedy occurred on the beaches where heavy shelling by enemy guns inland killed hundreds of troops. Despite the attacks, the evacuation was deemed complete by 1st June, with *Operation Dynamo* being downgraded three days later. Churchill called it 'a miracle of deliverance'. Over 338,000 troops, two thirds of them British, had been snatched from the jaws of death and capture. Though the military armour had to be left behind, the Royal Navy and the little ships had done their job well. In the House of Commons, Anthony Eden declared: 'Most of the BEF in Flanders, which the Germans claimed to have surrounded, have been saved. British troops have proved themselves superior to the Germans where they have met them.'

The vast influx of troops at the Channel ports meant that the Civil Defence organisation in Kent was working at full capacity. Many ambulances were commandeered from neighbouring counties to take the injured to hospitals. There were also other refugees. For one young woman, a Civil Defence driver in Folkestone, it was a period she would never forget as mentioned in the book, *Wartime Kent* by Oonagh Hyndman:

> On a beautiful, sunny afternoon, with a calm sea, our group was warned that a Belgian ship was due to dock at Folkestone. With several other girls, I took my ambulance down to the harbour where I saw a ship crowded with children, who had been moved from a hospital as German troops advanced. When we went below deck, there was a dreadful, sickly odour everywhere. We soon understood why. Almost all the children, from babies to those about twelve years of age, were stricken with a variety of diseases. Some needed stretchers, others were so thin and deformed that we just picked them up and gently carried them to the train waiting on the quayside. Our work was slowed down by air raid warnings and the occasional German plane zooming out of the haze. The ship had been at sea for two days – water supplies had practically run out so we got every container we could, filled it with water, and gave it to the refugees. Above all I remember, amid all that suffering, the wonderful calmness of the Sisters of Mercy who accompanied the ship and cared for the children. I often wonder what became of them all.

Once disembarked from the ships, both troops and refugees were put on trains. Most of them came up through Kent and, at many stations, the Civil Defence and the Women's Voluntary Service were there handing out tea and sandwiches. The people of Headcorn were to prove magnificent, as train after train stopped at the tiny station to allow 145,000 troops to enjoy their first decent meal in days. The same can be said of Paddock Wood, where the men were given clothes and boots, the result of house to house collections.

With Dover being the main port for disembarkation, 327 trains moved 180,982 troops, with Ramsgate coming a close second. Mention must be made that Southern Railway also rose to the occasion, with locomotives and carriages being pulled from all corners of the county. It was not only the trains that were requisitioned. At that time, the railway owned and operated most of the cross-Channel ferries. On 29th May all steamers over 1,000 tons came under military control. These included the *Lorina*, *Normania*, *Isle of Guernsey*, *Canterbury* and *Paris*. During several crossings and loaded with troops, the *Lorania* and *Normania* were sunk by bombing, most of

A superb painting of the evacuation of Dunkirk by Charles Cundall. (Kent Messenger -ref.PD1529099)

the crew and troops being rescued by other boats. Four days later the *Paris* was sunk, with much loss of life. H.R.P. Pratt-Boorman, then the owner of the *Kent Messenger*, the county paper of Kent, was to witness many of the returning boats:

> It was Wednesday, 29th May that I happened to visit Ramsgate. The seafront was crammed with people. They were watching the first arrivals of 335,000 soldiers, including wounded, who came ashore in small boats after being unloaded from larger boats out to sea. As they arrived they gave their names, dropped their rifles in a heap if they still had them, and

A train of Dunkirk troops get refreshment at Headcorn station.
(Kent Messenger -ref. 3042/6)

The late Henry Roy Pratt-Boorman and his wife Evelyn when he collected his CBE in 1966. (Kent Messenger -ref PD1073???)

climbed onto waiting buses or trains. They had come through hell. Tired, hungry and wet to the skin, they came in a steady stream for a week – yet always cheerful, glad to be home again. Next day, 30th May, I helped feed these returned men at Paddock Wood station and at Headcorn, where local residents hurriedly got together and cut bread and butter and made tea in field kitchens for trainload after trainload of men. What a godsend that bread and cheese, that fruit and those cigarettes were to them after days of hunger; and what tales they could tell of their last days abroad. One man commented, 'Never shall I forget the sound of the Navy's guns as we approached Dunkirk. It sounded as sweet to me as the bells of Canterbury Cathedral, my hometown. Thank God for the Navy.'

The entire Dunkirk operation cost Britain dearly in men and machines. A total of 68,111 men were killed, missing, wounded or taken prisoner. Some 2,472 guns,

Troops preparing road blocks as invasion threatens.

63,879 motor vehicles, 20,548 motorcycles and 679 tanks, together with tons of ammunition were lost or left behind on the beaches. A total of 243 ships were sunk whilst the RAF lost 474 aircraft.

The situation was grim, with Hitler just 21 miles away and already giving orders for an invasion. The nearest landfall was Kent. The county prepared for the worst, and bombing of the enemy-held French harbours took on a new meaning.

Such an operation took place over the night of 30th-31st May, when several Ansons from No 500 Squadron at Detling were detailed to carry out an operation code-named *Dundee*. One of the designated aircraft was MK-W, serial number R3389, crewed by Pilot Officer David Bond, Flying Officer Chambers (Navigator/Observer), Corporal Petts (Wireless Operator) and Leading Aircraftsman Smith (Gunner). Taking off at 23.00hrs, the aircraft successfully crossed the Channel and approaching the target, prepared to release its bombs. Unfortunately, the bomb release mechanism failed and despite renewed attempts, PO Bond realised that he must return to Detling with the bombs still on board. This was going to be highly dangerous and the crew prepared themselves for what they hoped would be a 'very soft landing'.

Crossing the English coast, one of the Cheetah engines began to splutter due to lack of fuel. With the aircraft losing height rapidly and the weather closing in, PO Bond was doubtful that he would even find Detling. However, through a break in the cloud, they saw that they were just a few miles away and prepared to land. Approaching on the final turn, the stalled engine suddenly burst into flames whilst the second engine, now starved of fuel, coughed and stopped. With a great deal of skill, PO Bond put the aircraft down on the grass runway but it landed badly and began to slide across the wet grass, out of control.

To Corporal Daphne Pearson, lying on her bunk in the WAAF quarters, it was not unusual to hear the Ansons splutter a bit when returning from a raid. On this particular night, however, she heard and saw something that was both terrifying and ominous:

> Hearing the crash I quickly pulled on some clothes and Wellington boots,
> seized my tin hat and ran out of the building towards the burning aircraft.

Detling sick bay staff with Cpl Daphne Pearson. (IWM)

After falling down an incline and over a bank, I arrived at the burning aircraft to see two men staggering about. One shouted, 'The pilot is still there, he's knocked out.' Seeing the ambulance arriving I told them to make their way to it whilst I rushed past them towards the aircraft. I was able to get quite close and saw the pilot still strapped in his seat. I managed to release him from his harness and drag him clear of the fuselage. As he regained consciousness he muttered that there were still bombs on board and that they would go up any moment. With all my strength I pulled him across the grass and down into the ridge that I had fallen into previously. Placing my tin hat on his head I pulled him down into the long grass. He murmured something about his face and I saw he had a lot of blood and a tooth protruding from his upper lip. I reassured him about his face and was attempting to remove the tooth from the wound when the plane blew up with a tremendous explosion. But for the ridge protecting us from the splinters of metal and the shock wave, we would both have perished. By now several other people had arrived on the scene, with further ambulances and fire engines, who were helping to put out the flaming grass all around.

Only when she was satisfied that she could do no more did Daphne leave the scene of carnage. Completely un-awed by her heroic deed, she wrote to her mother in Cornwall stating that she had been involved in 'a little something'. She wrote, 'My name has been sent to the King but I hope nothing will be done about it. When I read of the things our brave boys did at Dunkirk, my little bit is nothing at all.'

The King, however, had different thoughts on the courage of this brave WAAF. In June 1940, Daphne Pearson received her commission and the following month the *London Gazette* announced that Corporal (now Assistant Section Officer) Pearson had been awarded the medal that ranked next to the Victoria Cross, the Medal of the Military Division of the British Empire for Gallantry, the EGM. On a hot day in August she went to Buckingham Palace for the investiture – and ended up fetching water and caring for all of the men who fainted in the extreme heat. Again in 1941, she went back to the Palace to exchange the EGM for the George Cross. Lord Clarendon, the Lord Chamberlain, read from the official account of how Section Officer Pearson had saved the life of a seriously injured pilot of a crashed aircraft. The King told her: 'You are the first woman to win the George Cross. I congratulate you.'

With the end of the month, enemy activity began to increase. Hitler published his directive regarding invasion plans for England and the county stepped up its defence measures. It was none too soon, as the following chapters reveal.

Chapter 4

Preparing for Invasion

June to July 1940

With *Operation Dynamo* over, speculation about the prospect of a German invasion by sea and air was soon circulating. Reconnaissance photos showed a large concentration of barges and small craft in the harbours of Calais and Boulogne. This, together with the pace with which the enemy had conquered Europe, fuelled invasion thoughts in the county.

In preparation for such an event, all road signs were taken down and long poles strung with wire were erected in any sizeable grass area thought large enough to allow enemy gliders to land. Though we did not know it, Hitler had not initially wanted to invade England, he had seen the country as an ally to defeat Russia. However, he now thought we would not agree to his demands and so plans were made for an invasion. It was code-named *Operation Sealion*.

The work of defending our shores now took on a new pace. For the military, fresh units were being formed to defend the Kent coast, with large areas of what used to be pleasure beaches now becoming military hotspots. The *Kent Messenger* of June 1940 was paramount in keeping the population of the county informed of events:

> June was heralded by a bomb which fell on Lenham Congregational Chapel, demolishing it. It was at 4.30 in the afternoon of 1st June and half an hour after a host of school children had left. Rubbish, tiles and bricks from the chapel and neighbouring houses were strewn everywhere but no

one was hurt. Ashdown Forest caught it on 3rd June near, but fortunately far enough from a school evacuated there from the Medway Towns. In East Kent, everything has changed out of recognition. In guest houses such as Sea Views and Cliff Tops, where only recently holidaymakers had been staying, troops are now billeted ready to give Hitler a warm reception if he should dare to make a day's excursion to our shores. In the words of Mr Churchill, our people of the county are 'ready to fight on the oceans, on the landing grounds, in the fields and in the streets. We shall never surrender'.

These were stirring words and ones that gave encouragement to face the future.

Barrage balloons on Meopham cricket ground. (Kent Messenger -ref. PD1537227)

With Dover the closest point to the enemy coast, reinforcements were arriving all the time. Sapper Leslie Pearce recalled his change of scenery:

> I was a Sapper with No 502 Company, Royal Engineers, based at Chelsea Barracks, off Sloane Square in London. We were called up in September 1939 and transferred to Coastal Defence at Dover, with 519 Coast Battery Royal Artillery. A repair party of Royal Engineers was being formed, comprising some twelve tradesmen, fitters, electricians and drivers, together with a variety of trucks. The purpose of the staff was initially to install Lister 2½ ton diesel engines and generators along the coastline, with searchlights, to cover the Channel. Some 60 of these units were installed along the coast from Margate to Dungeness during April to August 1940. As I remember, there were engine replacements on the beaches at Dungeness, Lydd, Greatstone, St Mary's Bay, Dymchurch, Hythe, Folkestone and, in fact, all along the coast. At each site we trained Royal Artillery operators to use the equipment. We worked from dawn to dusk covering an area that was now closed to the public. The big generators gave enough power to illuminate the Channel for several miles in preparation for the expected German invasion.

Sapper Leslie Pearce, No 502 Company, Royal Engineers TA. His job was installing and maintaining searchlights along the coast between Margate and Dungeness. (Mr L. Pearce)

Defences at Maidstone Bridge, 1940.
(Kent Messenger -ref. 15202)

Gunners of the 90th AA Regiment deployed at Biggin Hill on Airfield Defence.

The King inspects the Dover defences, 13th April 1940.
(Kent Messenger -ref. 10/692/2/90)

Preparing for Invasion

The 163rd Battery of the Royal Artillery and the 55th Light Ack-Ack Regiment were tasked with defending Swingate and St Margaret's Bay, near Dover. Ted Cogdell, a dispatch rider with 163rd Batt RA Light AA Regiment, watched the destruction of several Channel ships during this warming up period for the Luftwaffe:

> There are so many memories of Dover, air raid after air raid, day after day. The 'Stand To' was one hour before sunrise and 'Stand Down' one hour after sunset. That, however, was not the end, as the sirens would go at any time of night or day. I was a despatch rider and whenever there was an air raid, I had to go out immediately to the gun sites, and when the raid was over, collect engagement reports. So more often than not I would be up on the cliffs looking over Dover and the Channel. What sights I saw! Perhaps it was the convoy of ships steaming through, ships carrying their own barrage balloons for protection. Then there were the screaming Stukas that would try to destroy the convoy or damage it. While this was going on, Hurricanes and Spitfires were doing their best to knock the enemy out of the skies. Vapour trails, dog-fights, the rat-tat-tat of the plane's guns and, of course, the dark bursts of 3.7" and 3" ack-ack. Two bombing raids I remember well include the raid in which the Stuka dive-bombers bombed one of our destroyers in the harbour. HMS Codrington was hit several times and sunk in the harbour itself. The other was when the Grand Hotel was hit. I know some people who worked in the hotel and had only been having a drink in the bar the previous evening. I thought to myself, 'There but for the grace of God, go I', as the hotel was quite demolished.

Within the county, the airfields and their squadrons were ready to repel and destroy any enemy aircraft that crossed our coastline. Biggin Hill, already battered and bruised by Dunkirk, received fresh squadrons to carry on the battle. Nos 32 and 79 Squadrons flying Hurricane 1s were glad to be back in the heat of the battle. Hawkinge, sitting on the cliffs overlooking Folkestone, was classified as a forward fighter airfield yet had no permanent squadrons in residence. This was because squadrons from the other airfields would fly down to Hawkinge at dawn, refuel and await an order to scramble before returning to their own bases at dusk. Flying from a forward airfield would allow them extra time in which to fight the enemy, even minutes were precious. The same can be said of Lympne, just inland from Hythe. Also classified as a forward airfield, several squadrons used it on a rotational basis.

Gravesend, the satellite airfield to Biggin Hill, had been fairly quiet since Dunkirk. Now it was to become a nightfighter base, with No 604 (County of Middlesex)

Auxiliary Squadron, flying the twin-engined Bristol Blenheim, in residence. Manston, on the Thanet coast, had also been home to squadrons participating in the Dunkirk operation but was now to become a very important fighter base and home to No 600 (City of London) Auxiliary Squadron. West Malling, still deemed as a satellite to Biggin Hill and Kenley (in Surrey) and a forward landing ground to Biggin Hill, was as yet unfinished and was to play only a minor role in the battle.

Detling, as we have read, was an important Coastal Command base. The same can be said of Eastchurch on the Isle of Sheppey, although faulty German intelligence believed them to be fighter bases. However, Eastchurch was now home to Nos 12 and 142 Squadrons, flying the Fairey Battle light bomber. Their primary duty was to bomb the barges in the French Channel ports, but this was not the only action in the Straits during June and July.

No 32 Squadron at Forward base, Hawkinge 1940. Left to right: PO R.F. Smythe, PO J.E. Procter, PO K.R. Gilman, Fl/Lt P.M. Brothers, PO D.H. Grice, PO P.M. Gardner, PO A.F. Eckford. (Author's collection)

No 610 (County of Chester) Squadron at Hawkinge. (Fox Photos)

*The Heinkel III shot down by PO Pain of No 500 Squadron flying an Avro Anson,
12th July 1940.*

Breakfast for ground crew at No 79 Squadron at Biggin Hill, July 1940. (RAF Museum)

At the same time as we were attacking the barges, the enemy were attacking British convoys in the hope of clearing the Straits of Dover. Before an invasion could begin it was necessary to establish air superiority and close the busiest waterway in the world to British shipping. A correspondent recorded in a war broadcast the flavour of one such event in florid terms:

> Well, now the Germans are bombing a convoy out at sea. There are several German dive-bombers, Ju 87s. These are now coming down on their targets, bombs gone. No, it missed. The enemy has not hit a single ship, there are about ten ships in the convoy but they have not hit a single one. Now the anti-aircraft guns are firing at them from the cliffs above Dover and, just overhead, the British fighters have arrived. Here they come in an absolute steep dive, Hurricanes with their guns blazing. And I can see one has hit a German, he's coming down in flames now. A long streak completely out of control. Now a parachute has left the aircraft, it must be the pilot of the Ju 87. There he goes, straight into the sea. SPLASH. A terrific wave of water and a success for one of our aircraft.

The softening up period had begun prior to the air battle becoming intense. With much of this initial fighting taking place in full view of the Channel ports, the MTB (motor torpedo boat) units stationed in Dover and other harbours were kept busy either rescuing downed airmen or attacking the harbours themselves. A.G. Floyd, Leading Stoker on MTB.70, part of the 11th MTB Flotilla at Ferry Dock Dover, remembers a hectic June and July in 1940:

> Just after Dunkirk, my boat, MTB.70, arrived at Dover as the nucleus of the 11th Flotilla. We were quite self-sufficient then, eating and sleeping on board between trips into the Straits. At first we used the Marine Harbour where HMS *Sandhurst* was based as a depot ship for the destroyers. Our duties were mostly patrolling the French coast at night and often we landed agents on the beach. We were spotted on one occasion and all hell broke loose but the sound of our engines roaring at full speed caused the searchlight crews to illuminate the sky looking for aircraft.
> We had so many incidents, one in full view of Dover Harbour. We had been picking up sailors from their sinking ships after they had been attacked by German aircraft, when we had to rush over to Calais to join two of the destroyers that had been attacking 'E' boats and escort them back to harbour. We were shelled from Calais but managed to keep out of their

range. On our return journey to Dover we were attacked by some Stukas. The two destroyers, *Boreas* and *Brilliant* were hit, as was MTB.69. We made smoke to allow the two destroyers to struggle back to Dover and it was not until we reached Dover that I smelt petrol on the mess deck. I lifted the floorboards to see fuel swishing around; the result was a hasty evacuation for we had also been hit in the petrol tank. We did further air sea rescues in the Channel but later the RAF had their own rescue service with High Speed Launches which took the heat off of us a little.

Hitler's War Directive No 16 stated: 'As England, in spite of her hopeless military position, has so far shown herself unwilling to come to any compromise, I have decided to begin preparations for, and if necessary to carry out, the invasion of England.' The directive was sent out to all his commanders in early spring 1940. By June, this was known to the British military and further plans were speedily put into action as the threat came ever closer.

In 1939 Churchill had described the aircraft warning system in the UK as 'early Stone Age'. The giant concrete listening slabs he referred to, at Greatstone and

Early listening mirror circa 1936 at Dover. (Author)

on the cliffs along the Kent coast, were certainly archaic. They were to be of no use for this conflict, but experiments in radar had progressed so fast that a good advance warning system was now in place. However, we still required a visual and audio system of aircraft reporting should this fail or be put out of action by enemy bombing. To meet the requirements a system that had its roots in the first conflict was extended to cover the whole of England and Wales. Known as the Observer Corps, this civilian aircraft identification service became part of the Air Ministry prior to the outbreak of war.

It was none too soon as the 30,000 Observers were mobilised and began to occupy the 1,000 reporting posts all over the country. The organisation was drawn up into groups with Nos 1 and 2 covering the Kent and Sussex coast and inland. Kent in No 1 Group had its headquarters in Maidstone, commanded by Mr J.H. Day. It was to here that the posts at Dungeness, Rye Harbour, Brooklands, Ham Street, Dymchurch and Folkestone would send information, being the first to report an advancing force whether by air or sea. This would then be filtered at the headquarters before being passed on to Biggin Hill, who would alert the squadrons on its airfields.

Air Chief Marshal Hugh Caswall Tremenheere Dowding, the AOC of 11 Group, stated that the function of the Observer Corps was to be the RAF's overland air-intelligence network for reporting aircraft. It certainly became that and more, as a seasoned Observer told me:

> The first Observer Corps group was Maidstone, followed by Horsham in Sussex. They were to cover the south-east of England but eventually groups covered the entire country. Observers could plot aircraft that radar could not and so the Corps played an essential part in the defence of the country. After the Battle of Britain, King George recognised the service of the Corps by giving it the title 'Royal', with a blue RAF uniform provided. Prior to 1940 the uniform was for Observer Corps Civilian Special Constables, a blue and white police arm band with Observer Corps woven on it. We had a room for talks on aircraft recognition and for rest between duties which, in the beginning, were in six four-hour shifts from 1 am. I became a full-time Observer for 48 hours a week.

Instructions for Observer Posts, published in 1934. (ROC)

The 350 ft high transmitting towers at Dover. (Air Ministry)

Though this photo was taken long after the Battle ended, it is a fine shot of Observers at their post.
(Kent Messenger -ref. PD1563994)

Our plotting machine had a circle measured off in squares: an inner distance sound circle of 5 miles and an outer one of 8 miles. A vertical bar in thousands of feet moved on a cog. This was the pointer which was on wheels and traversed the machine. It had a height correction pointer for distance over height and a torch for use at night. In the beginning, for practice, we used to plot British aircraft. Each aircraft was logged and a typical busy day might start with friendly bombers making a sortie to France escorted by a few fighters, and more would follow during the day. There were hostile raids by night which we had difficulty in plotting if the weather was bad. Later in the war a memo from ROC headquarters asked for volunteers to become aircraft identifiers on board ship. I volunteered and so I became a Seaborne Observer, which was very important over the D-Day landings.

In the countryside of Kent, the hops were beginning to climb the strings and farmers were busy growing extra crops, ably assisted by the girls of the Land Army. The colour khaki seemed to be everywhere in the county for, with the BEF safely returned from Dunkirk, defence became a priority. Many of those rescued from the beaches were back on duty after a spell of leave and some were put on airfield defence duties, including one member of the Princess Louise Kensington Regiment. Sydney Smith was on ground defence duties at RAF Lympne:

Having escaped from France via Cherbourg on 13th June 1940, the Kensingtons were reformed and took up positions in various parts of Kent to prepare for the threatened invasion. At one time 'B' company of the regiment took over the splendid house of Port Lympne, the one-time seat of Sir Philip Sassoon, as their HQ and billet. Our main duties were to guard the airfield with machine-guns to prevent landings by enemy paratroops and to intercept any sea-borne landings along the beaches from Hythe to Dymchurch.

We first arrived at Lympne after German dive bombers had already destroyed most of the hangars and much of the accommodation. There were one or two dummy Spitfires parked around the airfield but I do not really know if the young Luftwaffe pilots were entirely fooled. Just to tell you how poorly equipped we were, there was an old 1930s vintage lorry parked on the end of the airfield, on the back of which was built a concrete box, no top to it just sides. It could be driven onto the airfield to return fire from any attacking aircraft by firing out of the top with a Lewis machine gun. In Port

Lympne house a great roomy attic provided an excellent observation point from where we could see the dog-fights. Any aircraft that crashed, British or German, became our responsibility to guard until the salvage units arrived. I still look up at the house today and remember our time there.

Similar duties were being carried out at Hawkinge airfield by Mr H.V. Cussons who told me in 1990:

I was a private in the 70th Battalion The Buffs. We moved from St Mary's Bay to RAF Hawkinge in June. We were taken by lorries through country lanes and ended up at a place called Reinden House, tucked away in some woods, near the airfield. Although I lived at Ramsgate I'd never heard of it and certainly had no idea that within days it was to become a part of history. We became very busy preparing the defences, sandbagging and digging trenches, route-marching over miles of Kent and generally getting ready for what we knew would eventually come. The Buffs manned the gun pit near Gibraltar Lane after only two days' training on a Lewis gun. Nerves were so bad that anything approaching the airfield was fired at. I let rip at a plane once and must have frightened the pilot as he circled round to see who the culprit was. It was one of ours! I suppose at that stage of the war, friendly fire was inevitable.

Across the Channel, along the Pas-de-Calais, the Me109s of Jagdeschwaders 26 and 51 were being formed into what is best described as a 'hunting pack'. This became even more ominous due to the fact that JG26 was led by Major Adolf Galland and JG51 by Major Werner Molders. Both men had distinguished themselves as fighter aces during the Spanish Civil War, with Adolf Galland being quoted as saying, 'We had no illusions about the RAF. We knew it was an opponent we had to take very seriously.'

It was, however, not only the RAF that the enemy feared. On a clear day, from the coast of France, the Kent coastline was clearly visible. Over the Channel ports, large white objects could be seen floating in the air at heights of up to 2,000 ft. What the enemy was looking at were the balloons of No 961 Balloon Squadron who had responsibility for defending Dover. Whilst these balloons were frequently shot down by lone Messerschmitt Me 109s straying from attacking Channel convoys, they were quickly replaced and became a thorn in the side of the enemy. Hauptmann Hajo Hermann, the Commander of the 7th Staffel of Kampfgeschwader 30 came to fear them when, on one night-time mine-laying sortie along the coast, on 18th July, he came up against one as related in *The Luftwaffe War Diaries*:

> We had studied our maps carefully and thought that this would just be a routine operation. Coming in near Dover I throttled back and began my descent. Suddenly to my horror I saw a large sausage-shaped object silhouetted in the moonlight. It was a barrage balloon. I threw my Ju88 into a tight turn but it was to no avail. My controls felt sloppy and ineffective and I realised that we had collided with a balloon. With no speed as both of us began to fall together I ordered my crew to bale out. Suddenly we parted from the balloon and the controls began to obey my commands. I shouted to the crew to remain in the aircraft as we once again began to gain height. By now all the Dover ack-ack guns were firing at us but we managed to evade being hit. This was my first narrow escape and forever after I had a healthy respect for the balloon barrage.

Major Werner Molders, Commander of JG51 and one of Germany's greatest fighter aces. Killed November 1941. (ATB)

Hitting a balloon was a terrifying experience. Filled with highly inflammable hydrogen gas and low pressure, it had the ability to bring any aircraft down. Pilots of both sides came to respect their powers of destruction.

Down at the forward airfield of Hawkinge, 19th July 1940 was to become known as the day of the 'Slaughter of the Innocents'. On 12th July No 141 Squadron had flown into Biggin Hill from Turnhouse, near Edinburgh. Equipped with twelve Boulton Paul Defiant two-seat fighters, the squadron established its headquarters in the south camp of Biggin Hill, although the aircraft were to operate from the

A common sight in Kent: the balloon barrage flies over Dover.
(Kent Messenger -ref. 9/692/35/82)

Refuelling a Hurricane, No 32 Squadron at Hawkinge, July 1940.
(Fox Photos)

Women at work making barrage balloons. (Popperfoto)

nearly completed West Malling airfield. The Defiant had introduced a new tactical concept in fighters whereby no forward guns were fitted. All offensive fire power was concentrated in the rear cockpit by a four-gun, power-operated turret. No 264 Squadron had taken the Defiant into battle with spectacular results during the Dunkirk operation when they managed to shoot down 37 enemy aircraft. This was the result of the Luftwaffe pilots mistakenly identifying the Defiants as Hurricanes and diving on their supposedly defenceless tails.

The squadron was ready for operations by 18th July and the first scramble came the next day when the twelve Defiants flew to Hawkinge. By midday they were at readiness and were airborne by 12.32 pm, when only nine of the Defiants took off, engine problems keeping two on the ground whilst a third could not complete the take-off run. Assigned to patrol a line south of Folkestone at 5,000 ft, they noticed that down below them the Luftwaffe were attacking Dover. Flying in sections of three, line astern, the squadron were vectored to a point off Gris Nez when Fl Lt Loudon gave warning of enemy aircraft. Twenty Me 109s suddenly dived out of the sun.

The squadron broke to port and turned to deliver a beam attack. Unfortunately, the enemy pilots had by now realised that the most vulnerable part of this aircraft was the belly, where the guns of the turret could not bear down. In seconds, two Defiants were going down in flames into the sea. PO J. Kent and his gunner, Sgt R. Crombie, and PO R. Howley, with gunner Sgt A. Curley, were not seen again. Minutes later PO R. Kidson and Sgt F. Atkins were lost at sea. The slaughter continued as a fourth Defiant was hit. PO J. Gardner, although wounded, managed to bale out, whilst his gunner PO D. Slater was lost.

As the German pilots regrouped for a second attack, a fifth Defiant with Fl Lt M. Loudon and PO E. Farnes was hit in the engine. Diving to safety and although wounded in the arm, Fl Lt Loudon told his gunner to bale out as he attempted to reach Hawkinge. He crashed short of the airfield but survived, whilst PO Farnes landed in the sea and was picked up by an air-sea rescue launch. The carnage continued when a sixth Defiant crashed at Elmsvale Road, Dover, killing Fl Lt I. Donald, DFC, and PO A. Hamilton. A seventh aircraft, although damaged, managed to land safely back at Hawkinge. Tragically the pilot, PO I. McDougall had advised his gunner, Sgt J. Wise to bale out when the aircraft was hit. Although he landed in the sea and was observed to be swimming strongly towards the shore, Sgt Wise was never seen again.

For the Luftwaffe it was a triumphant action, even though they lost one aircraft. For No 141, its first action of the war had ended in tragedy, with six aircraft lost and four pilots and five gunners killed. The rest of the squadron were released from operations and were posted forthwith back to Prestwick in Scotland.

From Hawkinge it was possible to see the carnage taking place. The station intelligence officer at the time, PO H. Smith, recalled in the book, *RAF Hawkinge* watching the drama unfold:

> I kept them in view through my binoculars and when they were about mid-channel I saw the 109s swoop down. The Defiants had absolutely no chance against the German fighters and I watched in horror as they were picked off one by one and saw the splashes of water as they plunged into the sea.

For Captain Trautloft's 3rd Gruppe of JG51 operating from St Omer, the attack had been a triumph. Immediately after landing back at his base, he was called to a conference with Reichsmarshall Goering, the Luftwaffe commander, who stated: 'Fighting alone all these weeks on the Channel front has seriously weakened the British. Think now of all the bombers we can parade in the English sky – the few fighters they have left just won't be able to contend.' What he did not know was that 'Stuffy' Dowding was able to call on reserves from the other groups in different parts of the country.

Even though a lot of the fighting at this period was taking place over the Channel, Kent was being subjected to many raids. On 17th July a single plane dropped high explosive bombs on New Town, Ashford. One struck a shop in the Southern Railway Works which was busy making parts for aeroplanes, injuring several workmen. Further bombs were dropped at Lenham near Ashford. The enemy, however, did not have it all his own way. A German aircraft was shot down, landing in a hop garden at Collier Street near Maidstone. The farmer, driving his tractor, did not hear the dog-fight some distance away or the enemy aircraft crash. The first he knew was when the pilot landed by parachute in an adjoining field and walked over to him speaking very good English. Looking him up and down the farmer said, 'I suppose you had better come along to my house then.' He took the polite German home where his wife gave him a cup of tea until the police arrived to take him away. Chivalry was not dead after all! However, some of the enemy were not so lucky as Neville Bentley from Edenbridge recalled:

> In the summer of 1940 I was working at Fox and Manwaring, estate agents in Edenbridge, and one Friday there was a farm sale at Lingfield Lodge Farm, Marsh Green. It was a clear day and, in the afternoon, we saw and heard German bombers coming over escorted by fighter planes. Two Spitfires

A Dornier 17 rests in a hop garden at Marden in July 1940. (Kent Messenger)

were having a real dog-fight with a Dornier which was rapidly losing height. All of a sudden one of the crew baled out but the plane was too close to the ground and his parachute did not open. He landed about 200 yards from us, just inside the field where we were. My boss who was carrying a pistol went running up to the airman but he was dead so we covered him with his parachute. The Dornier crashed in the fields at the back of the farm and as far as I know any crew left inside were killed. Funny but I also recall that the German aircraft always seemed to come over on Sunday lunchtimes. We knew they were on their way because our dogs would start barking. Edenbridge had quite a few bombs dropped within the area and as a young man not old enough to join the forces it seemed an exciting time.

What has become known as the first phase of the battle was nearing its end. On 30th July, Hitler told Goering to have his forces in readiness to begin 'the great battle of the Luftwaffe against England' at twelve days' notice. The Luftwaffe had the false impression that they had superiority in the air but for many weeks few convoys had travelled through the Channel, allowing the RAF to gather its strength and recoup

Hermann Goering, Chief of the Luftwaffe. (Bundesarchive)

its forces. Even so, with the long, hot summer continuing, the demand upon Fighter Command, its pilots and aircraft, was beginning to take its toll. Yet no squadron diary or combat report reveals the strain that the RAF was under. The days were sixteen hours long, with three or four scrambles a day becoming commonplace. The last few days of July and the opening few days of August were to bring a lull but this was just the calm before the storm. To give a flavour of what the first phase of the battle was really like, I quote from the combat report of Sqd Ldr Worrall of No 32 Squadron based at Biggin Hill (from *RAF Biggin Hill*, Graham Wallace, 1957):

> I was leading Green Section on a convoy patrol off Dover from 17.00 to 18.00 hrs. At 17.40 Sapper [Biggin Hill control] told me Blue Section was joining me, also enemy aircraft between 10,000 and 20,000 ft were approaching the convoy. Almost at once I spotted them and ordering Green Section line astern, attacked the first Ju 87 just as he was starting his dive. Despite the fact that I had throttled right back I overtook him after a two second burst. I turned and took on another but had to break off as I was attacked by an Me 110. I then lost the 110 and saw the Ju 87s bombing

Pilots of No 610 Squadron at Hawkinge, 29th July 1940. (RAF Biggin Hill)

a destroyer. They finished bombing and made for home. I attacked the nearest who started smoking. I had to break off again as I was attacked by a 109. I could not see or find the 109 so attacked another Ju 87 which was near. I broke away. The 109 was not in view so I attacked a third Ju 87 which also started to smoke. I was just about to fire another burst when I saw tracer going over my port wing. I immediately broke away and felt bullets entering the aircraft from behind which were stopped by armour plating. Then two cannon shells hit, one in the engine and one in the gravity tank. I turned for home and the engine petered out just too far away from Hawkinge. I had to make a crash-landing in a small field half-mile to the east of the drome. Almost immediately she went up in a slow fire giving me about half a minute to get out.

On the last day of July, Fighter Command flew just 395 sorties, shooting down five enemy aircraft but losing three of their own in the process. The next phase, a more concerted one than before, was about to be unleashed upon the military and the civilians.

No 32 Squadron, Biggin Hill, July 1940 – two Polish airmen join the squadron, front row first and second from right, PO Pniak and PO Wlasndwalski. (RAF Biggin Hill)

Chapter 5

The Battle Begins

August 1940

The civil aspect of protection against enemy bombing and attack was primarily the responsibility of the police, the fire brigade and the air raid precautions (ARP) services. In 1940 these had separate identities, it was only in 1941 that they were all officially termed Civil Defence.

In 1936, the Home Office had published a booklet advising the public on how to protect themselves if and when war was declared. One extract reads:

> Street wardens will be required to act as guide and helper to the general public in the area to which they are allotted. It is particularly important that they should help to allay panic and give assistance to any families or persons in their districts, e.g. those who may have been driven out of their homes etc. They should help direct people in the streets to the nearest shelter. They should report to the police or the local intelligence centre the fall of bombs, dangerous fires, presence of gas, blocking of roads, damaged mains and any other information that may be required to enable a particular situation to be dealt with. They must be trained to give accurate reports and assess the situation.

In Kent during the war, when an incident occurred anywhere in the county, whether bombing, plane crash or shelling, it was reported to the Kent County Council

A typical street shelter in 1940. Even then humour had a part to play.
(Kent Messenger -ref. PD1536991)

The Medway Auxiliary Fire Service in action with fire barges on Rochester waterside. (Kent Messenger -ref PD1539694)

headquarters at Maidstone, the county town, where a log was kept. Wardens were issued with football rattles to warn of gas attacks if and when they came.

Fire-watchers would take up their posts each night to watch for the dropping of incendiary bombs. In 1940 the Auxiliary Fire Service (AFS) had not yet been formed into a National Fire Service. The equipment was basic with a single fire engine or small van towing a trailer pump which could be linked to nearby hydrants. If the main water supply had been cut off through bombing, water could be obtained from static tanks placed strategically at points around the county. If necessity is the mother of invention, then the AFS certainly were at the forefront. One unit in Horsmonden near Tunbridge Wells had the right idea, as the late Fireman Ernie Woods remembered when I interviewed him some years ago:

> A local fireman had produced an old Morris 6 saloon car which our crew converted. He cut the top right off and made it into a miniature fire engine with a manual pump on the back plus a cabinet place for the men to sit on. In the storage place we carried all the hose and 40 gallons of water. That was our complete unit. Our uniform consisted of boiler suits, a tin hat and Wellington boots and we carried three axes. The fire engine was kept in the old garage at the back of the King's Arm pub and our sleeping quarters were in the old stables there.

The Tubs Hill, Sevenoaks duty fire crew with van and trailer, 1940. (Author)

Something similar can be said of the Sevenoaks AFS in which my father served. Their van and pump was kept in the stables at the back of the Sennocke Arms in Tubs Hill in Sevenoaks. How well I remember him in his uniform (supplied late 1940), complete with axe hanging from his belt.

The contribution made by the Women's Voluntary Service (WVS) to civil defence must not be forgotten. Formed in 1938 to assist the ARP, they carried out numerous tasks from managing mobile canteens to manning switchboards in defence centres. They also helped to rescue people in bombed out houses, as a former WVS lady from Chatham recalled some years ago in the *Kent Messenger:*

My father, Jack Brooks, in the uniform of the Auxiliary Fire Service, 1940. (Author)

> We sometimes had to patrol for seven or eight hours at night whilst bombing was going on. They used to say women wardens were better than men because we knew what to look for. I would go into a house, find out who was alive, add up the number of victims and decide what to call in the way of fire services and ambulance. I was quite used to seeing dead people and not frightened by it at all.

The relatively quiet period from the end of July to the first week in August allowed the various branches of civil defence to become a cohesive organisation. This was none too soon as the brunt of the Luftwaffe attacks moved from the convoys and the English Channel much further inland. This period also allowed the enemy to reflect on their next move.

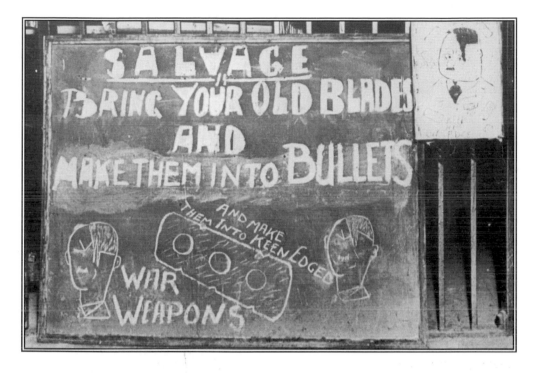

This notice was chalked up on Chatham railway station. It speaks for itself.

In early August 1940, at Cap Gris Nez, a high point on the French coast, two men were looking at the giant Dover radar masts through binoculars. Marshall Kesselring, the Commander of Luftflotte 2, one of the main units in the battle, and Reichsmarshall Goering chatted and laughed as they discussed the second phase of the attacks against England. Later that day, dressed in a white suit, Goering met all his commanders and repeated his broad objectives for the coming phase of battle. Once again emphasising air supremacy and the destruction of shipping in the Channel, he added that the destruction of the early-warning radar stations, once accomplished, would lead to the major assault on the airfields of the RAF.

The month of July had certainly given Dowding proof that the defensive measures in place would work. However, they had not yet been tested in the face of a heavy onslaught. The month of August was to prove just how good the system really was.

The first and second days dawned cold and dull, a contrast to the previous two months. Whilst the Luftwaffe waited for the better weather which was promised to arrive from the Azores within the next three days, Fighter Command was regrouping

Pots and pans make aircraft: one of the many piles to be turned into war machines. (IWM)

with a steady build-up in personnel and aircraft strength. On 3rd August, Dowding had 708 fighters available for operations and 1,434 pilots. Fifty-five squadrons were on strength, including Polish, Czech, Belgian, Free French and the American Eagle Squadrons. In addition six others were in training, including the Royal Canadian Air Force Squadron, No 1. With the threat of an invasion still prevalent, the entire country and especially Kent, knew that it would be a fight to the end.

On the Queen's birthday on Sunday, 4th August, all the stations played the National Anthem at first light. The Fighter Command Order of Battle stated that Biggin Hill had No 32 Squadron with Hurricanes and No 610 (County of Chester) Squadron with Spitfires in residence. The Hurricanes of No 501 (County of Gloucester) Squadron were at Gravesend and No 600 (City of London) were at Manston, with the twin-engined Bristol Blenheim.

Not until 8th August did a target present itself that was worthy of the enemy's attention. A large convoy CW9, code-named *Peewit*, had sailed from the River Medway the previous evening. Twenty merchant ships loaded with coal and coke for industry were escorted by a heavy naval presence. As the convoy entered the Straits, the German radar system plotted its progress. In the early morning it was attacked by E-boats from Calais, resulting in three ships being sunk, with two others damaged. Further raids followed and, by early evening, more ships had been sunk, leaving just four ships to sail into Swanage. It was a bad day for the Merchant Navy – but it was equally bad for the Stukas.

Flying a standard patrol, No 145 Squadron from Westhampnett in Sussex were airborne when vectored to a position near the enemy. They dived out of the sun for an attack. Sqd Ldr John Peel's jubilant, 'Come on chaps, down we go', sent the twelve Hurricanes wheeling down. In minutes the sky was full of whirling aircraft and the staccato sound of guns firing. In amongst the Stukas it was every man for himself as the relatively slow enemy aircraft fell to the guns of No 145 Squadron. Attempting to flee back home across the Channel, 19 Stukas did not return but sadly five Hurricanes were also lost in the fight, together with their pilots. Some have called 8th August the real beginning of the Battle of Britain. It was certainly when Fighter Command lost the greatest number of aircraft in a day since the start of the Channel offensive. Though Dowding and his commanders did not realise it, this was the prelude to what the Germans called 'Adlerangriff' or 'Eagle Day' – the start of an all-out effort by the Luftwaffe to destroy the RAF, both on the ground and in the air.

On the ground, 8th August also saw some of the first raids on Kent towns. In Maidstone, it was a normal Thursday morning with people going about their business as usual. Suddenly at 11.40 am the sirens around the town began to wail. People in the streets looked up and wondered if they should stay or make for the

Two casualties of the battle: Above, FO Lord Kay Shuttleworth, No 145 Squadron, killed 8th August 1940; Right, FO R.S. Demetriadi, No 601 Squadron, killed 11th August 1940, shot down in the Channel at 10.50 am. (ATB)

nearest shelter. Those in factories and schools did leave their premises and made their way to the safety of a shelter. For over 30 minutes, although aircraft engines were heard in the distance, no bombs fell. With the 'all clear' siren sounding at 12.30 pm, workers and schoolchildren returned to factory and schools alike, the latter pleased that several hours of schooling had been missed!

Two days later a lone Dornier Do 17 dropped bombs on the almost completed airfield at West Malling near Maidstone. No warning of the attack was given as the aircraft dropped from the cloud and in two runs over the airfield dropped 14 high explosive bombs. Seventeen workmen helping to construct the airfield were

seriously hurt, together with three Royal Engineer Sappers who received slight injuries. Several recently-built buildings were destroyed and No 26 Squadron, who had just moved in to the airfield, had two of its Lysander army co-operation aircraft hit. Bombs also fell at Wateringbury and the Leybourne Grange hospital. Luckily, the only casualty was a rabbit!

The 10th August was the day originally set by the German High Command for the commencement of 'Eagle Day'. However, changeable weather postponed the heavy attacks until the 13th. In between, there were attacks on the early warning radar stations.

Slightly inland at Rye, the Chain Home Radar Station was on full alert. The early morning watch had recently taken over and were firmly ensconced in the little wooden hut that served as the receiving room. Daphne Griffiths, one of the Corporal plotters, rubbed her eyes to get them accustomed to the glare of the cathode ray screen. The date was 12th August 1940. She had noticed in her diary that it mentioned 'Grouse shooting begins'. With a wry smile she wondered when her shooting would begin.

A similar pattern was being repeated at all the radar stations along the Kent and Sussex border. Pevensey, Dover, Fairlight and Dunkirk, together with Ventnor on the Isle of Wight, awaited the tell-tale blips of enemy aircraft. They did not have to

The Dover radar towers under attack, 1940. (Kent Messenger -ref. 738/14/76)

Radar operators in one of the Home Chain radar stations, 1940.
(Kent Messenger -ref. PD1456124)

Dunkirk Radar Station near Canterbury. (Kent Messenger -ref. 7/692/2/90)

wait long. At 9.25 am, Daphne noticed a blip of light suddenly appear indicating movement over Northern France. Calling the central Fighter Command filter room at Stanmore in Middlesex through her breast microphone, she reported, 'A new track at 30 miles. Only three aircraft, I'll give you a plot.' As she did so, across the Channel, the 3rd Staffel of Erprobungs Gruppe 210, with their leader Hauptmann Walter Rubensdoerffer were getting airborne in their Me 110s. Lifting off from Calais-Marcke airfield, the pilots could see clearly the Dover radar towers. In mid-Channel the force split with Rubensdoerffer setting a course for the station at Dunkirk, near Canterbury, Hauptmann Martin Lutz assigned to the Pevensey station, Oberleutnant Otto Hinze the fast-approaching Dover masts and Oberleutnant Wilhelm-Richard Roessiger the Rye station.

At Rye the instruction went out, 'Tin hats on, please.' Outside, the Bofors gun crew assigned to protect the station was at full action stations. Looking up, they saw three black dots diving down. Shouting to take aim, the commander, Major Mason, stirred his men into action. As the noise of the guns firing could be heard in the receiver hut, Daphne Griffiths began to shake with fear. Like most of the others in the hut, this was her first time under fire. Suddenly a different sound could be heard, that of screaming and exploding bombs as Roessiger unleashed his bomb load.

Although the explosions were deafening and frightening, the tall steel towers were left intact. Inside the hut, Stanmore repeatedly asked Daphne what was happening, only to receive no answer. She and the other plotters were sheltering under the table. Most of the glass windows had been shattered, throwing large slithers of glass everywhere. Dust and debris were falling all around as, outside, fire began to take hold of the undergrowth.

At Dunkirk, the bombs were accurate, destroying several buildings and moving one of the concrete blocks on which a steel tower stood. Yet again, the towers remained standing at all the stations despite the terrifying raids and remained on the air. What Goering had hoped for, that all the radar stations would cease to be operational by the end of the day, did not happen.

This was also the day that Dover and Folkestone first experienced a new type of attack, when they were shelled by the long-range enemy guns along the Pas-de-Calais. At around midday several loud explosions were heard, yet no aircraft were in the air. Suddenly several houses crumpled and fell to the ground as large shells dropped from the sky and exploded. This was a new and sinister type of shelling and one that the two coastal towns would become used to.

In other actions that day, No 610 Squadron at Biggin Hill were scrambled at 7.30 am to attack a high-flying formation of Do 215s. Sqd Ldr Ellis, the CO, reported

No 72 Squadron, Biggin Hill – ground crew assist a pilot to 'garb up'. (Central Press)

airborne and was vectored by the Biggin Hill controller to a point above Dungeness. With a call sign of 'Dog-Rose Red', he listened as further information came through his headset: 'Hullo Dog-Rose Red leader. Receiving you loud and clear. Vector 120 degrees. Nine bandits approaching Dungeness. Angels 10. Good hunting.' Later, came: 'Hullo, Dog-Rose Red leader. The bombers are all yours, leave the fighters to Bulldog Squadron.' Ellis answered, 'OK, received and understood.'

With a shout of 'Tally Ho', the twelve Spitfires fell upon the enemy. Ellis picked out one aircraft and, as it grew larger and larger in his sights, he pressed his gun button. He saw hits on the aircraft and followed it down as it went into a vertical dive towards the sea. Climbing back up he got another in his sights, fired and again had the satisfaction of seeing it fall. Looking down he could see his squadron in similar battles. For 20 minutes the battle raged, then suddenly it was all over. Eleven Spitfires returned to Biggin Hill whilst the rest of the enemy aircraft headed for France. (It must be remembered that the Luftwaffe only had a flying time of 15 to 20 minutes once over the English coastline before becoming low on fuel.)

A little later that morning Lympne and Hawkinge were attacked, causing considerable damage to both airfields although they remained operational. At the same time two convoys code-named *Agent* and *Arena* were off the North Foreland and the Thames Estuary. A force of Ju 87 Stukas attacked and sunk several ships. Spitfires from Manston arrived too late to prevent further damage but it was No 501 Squadron from Gravesend that suffered major losses, with one Hurricane lost with its Polish pilot, FO K. Lukaszewicz killed, and three further Hurricanes badly damaged. At 12.50 pm the Luftwaffe were over Kent again, when 18 Do 17s bombed and strafed Manston airfield. This was a major attack destroying many buildings and putting giant holes across the landing area, leaving it non-operational. Two Blenheims of the resident No 600 Squadron were badly damaged but although the devastation was immense, there was no loss of life.

A Crossley refueller fills a Spitfire of No 66 Squadron at Gravesend in 1940. (The Times)

A posed photograph depicting scrambling
pilots, thought to be Hawkinge in 1940.
(Fox Photos)

On this particular day, it was not only the RAF that had suffered but also the civilian population of the county. A stray bomb from a raider that had wandered inland fell on Bekesbourne, killing six people, with one serious injury and another person slightly injured. Houses and roads were also damaged by 250 high explosive and incendiary bombs. Ronald Blay, who still lives at Ramsgate, recalls:

> In August the German planes with big black crosses would come over dropping bombs and also strafing with machine guns. One night we were on our way to the shelter when a German came over with his guns blazing, tearing slates off the house nearby. We flung ourselves to the ground and were terrified. Another time the air-raid warning went and we took to the Anderson shelter listening to the huge bangs getting closer when everything shook the air. When we came out, a bomb had dropped 20 yards away. We were lucky because the next time we came out of the shelter the air-raid wardens' thick concrete shelter a short distance away had taken a direct hit, killing some of my friends.

That night German radio gave jubilant news of their success. They reported heavy damage on the mainland and claimed 71 RAF aircraft, including the entire No 65 Squadron at Manston, were damaged beyond repair. They further claimed that 46 Spitfires and 23 Hurricanes had been destroyed the previous day. Whilst the attacks had been severe, it was just a foretaste of what was to come.

The 13th dawned mainly fair, with early morning mist and slight drizzle. Along the French coast, Luftflotten 2 and 3 were ready for the big attacks. Generalfeldmarschall Albert Kesselring and Generalfeldmarschall Hugo Sperrle, the two commanders, were digesting a signal just received from Reichsmarschall Goering. It read: 'Operation Eagle. Within a short period you will wipe the British Air Force from the sky. Heil Hitler.'

By 7.15 am German bombers were crossing the Channel. However, since dawn the weather had deteriorated and a personal signal from Goering postponing the first attack was sent. Not all units received the signal in time, and were already airborne by the time it was sent. Another problem was that due to different types of radio, the bombers and fighters could not communicate with each other. The Me 110s that were to escort the Do 17s did receive the recall signal and frantically flew alongside Colonel Joachim Huth in one of the bombers in the hope of attracting his attention by sign language. This did not work and whilst the Me 110s returned to base, the main force of 74 bombers from KG2 ploughed on heading for their target, Eastchurch on the Isle of Sheppey. Once again, faulty German intelligence had been led to believe that Eastchurch was a fighter base. True, it actually did have a temporary Spitfire squadron in residence, No 266, but the airfield was assigned to Coastal Command.

Crossing the estuary, the low cloud dispersed and the pilots of KG2 could clearly see Eastchurch. Suddenly, No 74 Squadron from Hornchurch appeared on the scene, together with No 111 Squadron from Croydon and No 151 from North Weald. Four Do 17s were shot down instantly, with a further four damaged. This did not stop the rest of the enemy aircraft attacking Eastchurch, however. One of the pilots from No 266 Squadron described an early morning wake-up call in an HMSO booklet published during the war:

> I awoke to find my bed being thrown around all over the place. Not quite realising what was happening I tried to sit up but found that every time I fell back down again. The entire hut shook, glass was flying everywhere so I thought I would stay put as it was the safest place. The noise and explosions seemed to go on for hours but was really only minutes. When I did finally manage to get out of bed I looked through broken glass and saw total carnage. Fires seemed to be everywhere, with people running about not quite knowing just what to do.

Eastchurch had received a direct hit on the operations room, putting it out of action. Five Blenheims of resident No 35 Squadron were destroyed, with many Spitfires of No 266 Squadron reaching a similar fate. Sadly, twelve people were killed, with a further 40 injured. Despite the devastation, however, it in no way affected the performance of Fighter Command. Thus, the efforts of KG2 were of little use in helping to clear the skies of British fighters. Just how faulty the German intelligence network was is further amplified when later that day another raid, although with dire consequences, was also made on a Coastal Command base.

The Detling Operations Record Book for 13th August 1940 states in dispassionate terms: '16.05hrs – aerodrome attack by German aircraft. Severe damage caused, including direct hit on ops room.' It was the day when the Luftwaffe attempted to wipe Detling from the face of the earth.

The station had been relatively quite all day. Several air-raid warnings had been issued with the correct colour codings but none lasted long. However, at 4 pm colour coding turned red as 86 Ju 87 Stukas escorted by Me 109s appeared out of the cloud over the airfield. Shrieking down, the Stukas achieved the measure of surprise they needed. On the ground many of the men and women were either walking to the mess for tea or were already sitting down when the first bombs fell.

This Dornier 17 crashed at Barham near Canterbury on 13th August 1940. Its remains lie across the Canterbury/Folkestone railway line. (Associated Press)

The accuracy of the raid was deadly. Every part of the grass landing area was hit, causing huge bomb craters and throwing earth and rocks high into the air. Fires were started in all the three hangars, eventually spreading to enormous proportions and destroying 22 aircraft. A direct hit on the semi-sunk, bomb-proof operations room caused the entire concrete ceiling to fall in, killing the station commander, Group Captain Edward Davis, a former tennis champion. He fell to the ground with a piece of jagged concrete driven straight through his skull.

As the Stukas spread death and devastation at Detling, the local population wondered just what had hit them. Casualty Clearing Officer Wallace Beale, a Maidstone undertaker, sped to the shattered airfield, together with local units of the Civil Defence. The scene they found would have made many a weaker man ill. Of the 67 people killed, many needed only the 5 ft coffins reserved for unidentified remains. A further 94 were injured and many of them could not be treated in the station sick bay. A fleet of ambulances arrived to take those badly injured to Preston Hall hospital, including many army personnel who were on airfield defence duties. The complete surprise of the attack had shocked the servicemen and women, as the late Sqd Ldr S.W. Jarvis recalled when I interviewed him some years ago for my book on No 500 Squadron:

> On 13th August I was on the staff at the station headquarters which comprised a group captain commanding officer, a squadron leader administration, the adjutant, the assistant adjutant who was myself and two junior WAAF officers. On this particular day the squadron leader 'A' was off-duty, also the two WAAF officers. During the afternoon the CO and the adjutant went together to the operations room leaving me as the only officer in the station headquarters.
>
> Suddenly I heard the sound of an aircraft approaching at high speed and very low. Thinking that it must be one of our own planes returning to beat up the station, I was surprised to see the explosions of bombs on the roof of the operations room as I was walking across the room to look out. Fortunately the window was shut otherwise I should probably have been killed by the blast as the explosions were only about 30 yards away. Even so, the glass shattered and I ran across the other side of the room. Just then the station RED air-raid warning commenced to sound so I rushed off to prevent any of the office staff from attempting to go to the air-raid shelters whilst bombs were still falling around. For the majority of the people on the station this was their first taste of being under fire and, being an old hand, I had to rush round and restrain them from going outside and

becoming further casualties. As soon as the station 'all clear' sounded, the ambulances were quickly on the scene where two doctors joined them.

One of the first things I did was to phone the operations room to enquire after the CO and adjutant. Not being able to get through I walked the short distance and was told that both of them were dead. It was ironical really as the operations room had been considered to be the safest spot on the station, with a special bomb-proof roof. The officers' mess was badly damaged, putting it out of action. However, the senior WAAF officer informed me that her girls had asked her to invite the officers to use the half of their dining room which was not being used by them at present. Accepting their offer I went outside to see how the station warrant officer was getting on organising parties to clear up the wreckage.

The doctors had examined every casualty, the dead were left where they were but, where possible, the others were moved to a convenient place to await further ambulances. It was necessary to collect the dead and line them up in a clear spot ready for the undertaker. As some of them were rather unsightly, I told the warrant officer that I would take that job over myself if he could find half-a-dozen men who were willing to assist me. We had no stretchers available as they were all being used for the living casualties, therefore the dead had to be carried three or four men to each body as required. Some of the bodies had parts of their arms or legs blown off; we made a small pile of limbs that we found and left it to the undertaker to sort them out if he could. When we had finished transporting the bodies to a piece of land near the main gate we covered them all with blankets, including the pile of limbs, and departed to have a welcome hot drink in the WAAF mess. We had left behind 36 bodies and one pile of unknown parts.

Soon after the raiders had left, Group headquarters rang up to ask what the situation was. A few minutes later the Air Ministry rang with the same question. Each was given a brief account and name of the senior wing commander who would act as CO until a replacement was posted to the station. This day was to become the worst of my life, one that I shall never forget.

Sqd Ldr Pain saw the death and destruction from the air:

I had taken off earlier that afternoon to carry out a reconnaissance over the Channel. As we made our way back at around 3.30 pm I said over the intercom to the crew something that turned out to have remarkable prescience, 'Detling is going to catch a packet today.' No one else spoke. Whilst over the Thames Estuary we found a wrecked ship and decided to have some front gun practice on it. I had shot down a He III with my front gun the previous 12th June so we regarded ourselves as rather superior to Hurricanes, if not quite up to the standard of Spitfires! We then set course for Detling.

As we approached, the sky clouded over, 10/10ths at 3,000 ft. There also seemed to be something strange about the airfield – scars of yellow earth all over the surface. Then the hangars – good God! They looked rather like badly damaged kitchen colanders. It was unbelievable that this could really happen to our home. It was most unfair! Still, it was war. We sailed slowly around the circuit noting the damage. The ops room had obviously taken a direct hit right in the centre. All the messes had been blown to bits, with the exception of the WAAF one. We turned finals and landed very carefully, picking our way through the craters that covered the airfield and taxied back to 'A' flight dispersal. We had missed the whole show because of our dallying on our return. How lucky can you be!

As evening approached, the situation became more manageable. Plans were made to evacuate the WAAFs and some of the non-essential personnel to outlying houses, leaving just the duty and aircrew people at Detling. The sick bay was moved

The mass funeral after the 13th August 1940 raid on Detling airfield.

The Commonwealth War Graves Section in Maidstone Cemetery. It contains many of the victims of the 13th August 1940 raid on Detling, also the German crew of the Tonbridge Road incident.

out to a big house on the Sittingbourne road called Woodlands.

Later in the week a mass funeral was held at Maidstone cemetery for the majority of the dead. This was another harrowing experience for all those who attended, with the great yawning trench, the dozens of service lorries and the seemingly unceasing chain of coffins. The funeral bearers, a number of them drawn from the resident No 500 (County of Kent) Squadron, struggled and stumbled across the uneven grass. Large groups of weeping relatives and friends attended to pay their last respects to the dead. Many had travelled long distances to be there. The station padre and several civilian clergy read the funeral service and finally the dead were buried in peace. Somehow, life at Detling would never be the same.

Later that year the Military Cross was awarded to PO D. Elliot who had helped

Josie Fairclough with her Dame Laura Knight portrait. She was awarded the
Military Medal at Detling on 13th August 1940. (IWM)

rescue some of the injured in the operations room. A Military Medal was awarded to Corporal B. Jackman, one of the army men on airfield defence who stayed firing his twin Lewis gun at the Stukas until a nearby bomb wrecked the gun post. Two WAAFs were decorated for bravery under intense fire: Corporal Josie Fairclough, (née Robins) was awarded a Military Medal for assisting in helping the injured when a shelter full of personnel was hit, whilst Sgt Youle was also awarded the Military Medal for staying at her post in the telephone exchange and calmly informing group headquarters what was happening. The citation for both women stated: 'They showed extreme courage with calmness and efficiency at a most dangerous time for all.'

Slowly, the airfield got back to normal. Elsewhere in Kent two people had been killed by bombs at Whitstable and two more killed on Sheppey. At the end of the day, everyone knew that the Battle of Britain was well and truly on.

The next day, 14th August, cloud kept enemy action to a minimum. Even so, No 610 Squadron from Biggin Hill tangled with a mixture of Stukas and Me 109s off

Folkestone, claiming six confirmed and seven probables. Fighter Command lost three Hurricanes. Bombing by further Stukas sank the Goodwin Sands Lightship and several barrage balloons were shot down at Dover. This was a day that Leading Aircraftsman Timperley of No 961 Balloon Squadron remembers:

Of course, there were the usual air-raid warnings, the shell warnings, the all-clear and the air-raid warning. One day, I think it was a Saturday, the Germans came over and shot all the balloons down. I think there was a total of 23 altogether. It started around 8 am but we had plenty of spare balloons so it was just a case of firing them up and sending them aloft. Once again at noon, they came back and shot all of them down again. Up went some more and then, at around 5 pm, back they came and shot those down as well. However, by dusk, we had them flying again and the next raid was intercepted by Spitfires so they did not have the chance to get near them. We worked entirely in the harbour on barges and buoys and on the Eastern Arm servicing and flying balloons from out of Granville Dock. It was a wonderful experience with hindsight and there were many civilians who remained to give a good example of courage to us

Biggin Hill 1940 – the Salvation Army tea wagon visits. (RAF Biggin Hill)

all. They used to bring the Salvation Army tea wagon down to us and not even shelling or bombing could stop them.

And so, as 15th August dawned, many of the airfields prepared for a new onslaught. This time it was Hawkinge and Lympne that received serious attacks. The early hours were unusually quiet. At Biggin Hill both squadrons were at 15 minutes' readiness whereas No 501 had left Gravesend at dawn and were waiting at Hawkinge for a scramble. That came at 11.30 am. Patrolling high above the airfield they failed to see a force of Stukas approaching from the east. The airfield defence gunners did see them and were busy firing at the armada as it approached but rather too late to do any damage and the Stukas had it their own way. Screaming down from the sky, they dropped their 1,000 lb bombs on the one hangar that still stood. It disappeared in a cloud of fire and smoke, along with a barrack block. The landing area became a field of craters, with fragments of bomb casing flying everywhere. Lympne suffered a similar fate, with the station sick quarters and other buildings demolished. Worse

The Stuka crash of Unteroffizier Weber on 15th August 1940 at Shorncliffe Crescent, Folkestone. Gunner Franz Kraus was also killed.

still was the fact that all water and power supplies were cut off leaving the fire service to battle the fires with very little water. This picture of attacks was carried out all over the country as far north as Sunderland.

Back down south, it was the turn of Manston to suffer a heavy onslaught. Twelve Me 109s attacked with cannon and machine guns, destroying two Spitfires and causing 16 casualties. The aircraft manufacturing plant of Short Brothers situated at Rochester also received the second of several attacks. It was here that the company was busy producing the first four-engine bomber for the RAF, the Short Stirling. Although 3,000 personnel were working at the factory at the time, only one death occurred. This was because a system of trenches and shelters had been dug around the perimeter of the airfield, giving the workforce a relatively safe shelter. However, six completed Stirlings were destroyed, as well as tools and valuable machinery. The raid caused the production of the Stirling to be suspended until 1942 and then it only restarted on a limited scale, with the manufacture of certain parts spread around the Medway towns.

Two further attacks came in the early evening. Again the airfields were caught off-guard as aircraft were on the ground refuelling and re-arming. Making for Biggin Hill, the Germans spotted West Malling and mistook it for their target. Runways and buildings were badly damaged once again.

A further assault on Hawkinge found No 32 Squadron doing battle over the coast. The German pilots pushed through their attack with courage, twisting and rolling out of the opposing gun sights. Several parachutes were seen to open and float gently down only to land in the sea; rescue was carried out by the air-sea rescue launches. The noise around Folkestone and Dover was indescribable. Screaming aircraft engines, exploding bombs, the staccato sound of machine gun bullets and the shouting of men and women under attack.

After intense fighting over the whole of southern and eastern England, dusk brought peace and quiet. Both sides counted their losses. The RAF had lost 32 fighters, with 28 damaged but repairable. Thirteen pilots had been killed, with ten in hospital. The enemy had lost 72 aircraft, with 165 aircrew killed or taken prisoner. Amongst the dead was Hptm Rubensdoerffer, the commander who had carried out the first attacks on the radar stations.

That night the BBC 9 pm news bulletin reported victory for the RAF. Many aircrew from Nos 32 and 610 Squadrons heard the news in the bar of the White Hart in Brasted, a favourite watering hole for the Biggin Hill squadrons and just a stone's throw from the airfield. Swapping stories of success or failure and thinking of lost comrades, the pilots forgot the tragedy of war for a few hours at least. With a shout of 'Last orders, gentlemen, please' from landlords Teddy and Kath Preston, they

The famous 'pilot signature' board in the White Hart pub at Brasted, the watering hole for Biggin Hill squadrons. Licensee Mrs Kath Preston points to the signature of Wg Cdr Mike Crossley (No 32 Squadron) in September 1969.

stumbled back to Biggin Hill to sleep until dawn when once again they would be back on duty. Outside in the cold light of dawn, the ground crews were working feverishly to get as many Hurricanes and Spitfires as they could back into service. Theirs was an onerous task and one that every pilot knew his life depended upon; as such, one depended on the other.

Next day the newspapers were full of the success of the RAF in shooting down so many enemy aircraft. In large black headlines they all praised the courage and tenacity of the pilots and the men who serviced the aircraft. For Robert Stanford Tuck, already on his way to becoming an ace, the days of that long, hot summer would enable him to become the very epitome of a fighter pilot, with his check scarf wrapped around his neck and tucked into his tunic. His biographer, Larry Forrester, recorded just one of Tuck's encounters with the enemy in his book, *Fly For Your Life* (Panther 1959):

He had the sudden unsettling conviction that this one was different from all of the others. This one was more dangerous. It wasn't going to stop firing at him, it wasn't going to break off no matter how much lead he pumped into it. This one could be death.

All this was happening, all these thoughts and feelings were crowding on him, in the space of a mere two or three seconds. But everything was so clear, so sharply focused. The moment seemed to stand still, in order to impress its every detail on his mind.

The silhouette grew and grew until it seemed to fill the world. He clenched his teeth and kept firing to the last instant – and to the instant beyond the last. To the instant when he knew they were going to crash, that each had called the other's bluff, that they could not avoid the final terrible union.

Then it was a purely animal reflex that took command, yanked the stick over and lashed out at the rudder. Somehow the Spitfire turned away and scraped over the bomber's starboard wing. There could have been only a matter of inches to spare, a particle of time too tiny to measure. Yet in that fleeting trice, as he banked and climbed, showing his belly to his foe, several shells smashed into the throat of the cowling and stopped up the Spitfire's breath. The elaborate systems of pipes and pumps and valves and containers which held the coolant and oil, and perhaps the oil sump too, were bent and kneaded into a shapeless, clogging mass that sent almost every instrument on the panel spinning and made the Merlin scream in agony...

It was an awkward fall and he wrenched a leg and was severely winded. He was in a field just outside the boundaries of a house called 'Plovers', the lovely, old-world estate of Lord Cornwallis at Horsmonden. Several people had seen his spectacular arrival and witnessed his Spitfire crashing a few hundred yards away in the open Kent countryside. An estate wagon arrived to take Tuck to the house where his Lordship had already prepared a bed and called his personal physician. But Tuck, once he had stopped vomiting, insisted on getting up to telephone his base – and once on his feet would not lay down again. He had a bath leaving a thick coat of oil on his Lordship's bath tub and despite the doctor's orders, borrowed a stick and hobbled downstairs to join the family for tea. However, exhaustion took over and helping him back upstairs, Tuck fell asleep for seven hours. When he awoke, his Lordship's son was waiting to take him back to Biggin Hill. 'Drop in for a bath any time, m'boy,' called his Lordship as the car sped off.

The next two days saw further bad attacks on the airfields. West Malling was hit again by bombs, rendering it unserviceable. In the 24 hours of the 16th, the Luftwaffe put up 1,715 sorties for the loss of 45 aircraft. The RAF lost 22 fighters and sadly lost eight pilots.

It was during an enemy attack on Gosport airfield near Portsmouth that Fl Lt James B. Nicholson of No 249 Squadron won Fighter Command's first and only Victoria Cross of the battle. Leading Red section of the squadron, the Hurricanes were vectored to patrol between Poole and Romsey at 15,000 ft. Whilst climbing to 17,000 ft the section was bounced by enemy aircraft in an attack which came out of the sun. All three aircraft were hit by enemy fire. Fl Lt Nicholson, his cockpit a mass of flames, unstrapped himself and prepared to bale out. As he did so, he saw an Me 110, possibly the one that had attacked him. Although in great pain, Nicholson attempted to do battle with the enemy who was twisting and turning in an effort to escape him. Badly burnt,

The Victoria Cross of Fl Lt James Nicholson.
(ATB)

Nicholson finally managed to bale out and as he floated down on his parachute, he saw the skin on his hands simply hanging off. Landing heavily and in great agony, he was taken to the Royal Southampton Hospital and later transferred to the RAF hospital at Halton. After treatment for his burns, including several operations, he then went to convalesce at Torquay. On 24th November 1941, he went to Buckingham Palace to receive his VC. Promoted to Wing Commander, he sadly did not survive

Fl Lt James Nicholson talks to the Matron in the convalescent home.
(Fox Photos)

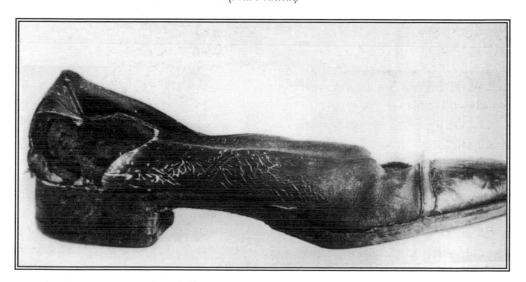

Fl Lt Nicholson's left shoe damaged by the cannon shell.

the war. On 2nd May 1945, he died when the Liberator he was travelling in crashed in the Bay of Bengal. He was just 29 years of age.

With a slight lull on the 17th due to changeable weather, it was time for Fighter Command to take stock. The serious drain on pilots was recognised by Dowding and the Air Ministry, the result of which was that the AOC requested that Fairey Battle pilots fill the gaps. However, the Air Staff felt that to do this would seriously affect the striking force of the light bomber squadrons. After further discussion, a compromise was reached: five volunteers from the four Battle squadrons and three each from the Army Co-op Lysander squadrons would join Fighter Command. There was no shortage of volunteers. Leaving their regular units, they were sent to an OTU for six days and carried out their first operational patrol within a fortnight.

Sunday, 18th August 1940 became known as 'the hardest day'. This was the culmination of a week's all-out effort by the Luftwaffe to destroy Fighter Command, when massed formations returned to attack Kenley, Croydon, Biggin Hill, Manston and West Malling. A visit by Anthony Eden to ravaged Hawkinge on that day enabled him to see first-hand just what war on the front line was like. By midday over 300 enemy aircraft were in the sky above Kent. One of the worst assaults was on Biggin Hill, an attack that by dusk would see the airfield nearly out of action. Never before had the enemy made such a determined effort to wipe out the RAF.

First, however, it was the turn of Kenley in Surrey to be bombed. This was a devastating attack which left the airfield in ruins. Then, shortly after 2 pm it was the turn of Biggin Hill. Heinkel He IIIs, Dornier Do 17s and Junkers Ju 88s, with an escort of Me 109s, crossed the coast and flew inland. The 15 Spitfires of No 610 Squadron were already airborne by this time, whilst twelve Hurricanes of No 32 Squadron were rolling down the runway. On the ground, all non-essential personnel were taking to the shelters as the sirens began to sound throughout the area. Many staff left their Sunday lunch to take shelter as the station commander, Gp Cpt Richard Grice, spoke over the tannoy: 'This is your station commander. At any moment we may be attacked. I want all personnel except those engaged on essential services to take cover.'

It was none too soon. As the first of the enemy aircraft, the Do 17s, crossed the airfield threshold, the Parachute and Cable system (PAC) was fired. This was an airfield defence system that launched a rocket, the warhead of which contained a parachute and a length of cable. When the rocket reached its designated height, the warhead exploded, releasing the parachute and cable which would then float back down to earth. In the process, it was hoped that it would entangle itself in the engine of an enemy aircraft. Though a somewhat precarious device, in the case of Biggin Hill it worked as two Do 17s immediately crashed to the ground.

Both Biggin Hill squadrons were now engaging the enemy in sight of the airfield, together with the heavy guns of the 58th Heavy Ack-Ack Regiment on airfield defence. This tended to split the enemy formations, a consequence of which was that many bombs fell on the surrounding area. One particular Do 17 ventured low on its approach to the airfield. Already damaged, the aircraft was further hit by aircraft from No 111 Squadron, the ground defences, plus a fusillade of shots fired by the local Home Guard. Coming over Leaves Green, the Dornier burst into flames and crashed just short of the airfield. As the four crew members scrambled out, the local Home Guard platoon were celebrating the fact that they had played a part in shooting them down. The platoon commander gave his verdict: 'I gave the order to fire and we pumped 180 rounds into the belly of the bomber. When it came down, the crew got out and looked very arrogant. Typical blond Germans!'

Arrogant or not, there is no evidence that the Home Guard alone shot down the aircraft, more it was a combination of fire from the Hurricanes of Sgt J. Dymond and Brown of No 111 Squadron, the airfield defence and the Home Guard. The German crew were taken to hospital in Bromley before being transferred to a POW camp in Canada.

The raid on Biggin Hill lasted barely ten minutes but in that short time the airfield became littered with bomb craters and unexploded bombs. A Bofors gun crew pit was hit, killing one gunner and injuring several others. In addition, the MT sheds were damaged.

There is, however, a tale of exceptional courage in the face of intense attack. Sgt Joan Mortimer, a WAAF telegraphist, was manning the switchboard in the armoury and although surrounded by tons of high explosive, refused to leave her post. Her duty entailed passing information to the various defence units guarding the airfield. Although terrified by the sounds of exploding bombs and intense gunfire, she coolly carried on her duties, and when the all clear sounded, she went outside to assist in placing red flags where bombs were seen to have not exploded. Even one exploding close by did not deter her. Joan Mortimer's brave actions resulted in the award of the Military Medal, the first of three such medals to be awarded to members of the WAAF at Biggin Hill.

Later that afternoon, a large force of enemy aircraft was met over the town of Ashford by the Hurricanes of No 56 Squadron flying from North Weald in Essex. Patrolling at 22,000 ft, one of the pilots spotted five Me 110s flying as though they had become detached from the main force. Tearing into them, the Hurricane pilots shot them all out of the sky. None of the pilots were able to

Sgt Joan Mortimer – her citation told of 'exceptional courage under fire'.
(RAF Biggin Hill)

bale out. In contrast, hours later, PO Kenneth Lee, one of eight fighter pilots that day to take to his parachute, landed at Whitstable. The reception he received was far from friendly, as he recalled in *The Battle of Britain* by Hough and Richards:

> Having been shot down and lightly wounded, I was taken to a local golf club, just inland from Whitstable, to await an ambulance. I was in shirtsleeves, slightly bloodstained, but couldn't help hearing members at the last hole complaining that the distraction of the battle in the air was disturbing their putting. Even worse was heard when, once inside, a voice demanded, 'Who's that scruffy looking chap at the bar? I don't think he's a member.'

The next day, the *Kent Messenger* reported the day's fighting in glowing terms:

> In East Kent hundreds of planes were in the air dog-fighting. A large enemy formation was split up by our fighters and then the real fight began. Each one seemed to select an opponent and bring him down. Planes seemed everywhere in all parts of the sky, fierce combats took place. Occasionally the 'crump' of bombs showed the Nazis were getting the worst of it and were anxious to drop their bombs and leave as soon as possible. On the ground everyone tried to look all ways at once with remarks such as 'There goes another one, look' and 'Did you hear that crump?'. One of the many Nazi pilots was captured by Platoon Commander E. F. Talbot of the Home Guard in Maidstone. He rounded him up, disarmed him and then said, 'Spitfire got you. Spitfire good.' The German, still in fighting mood replied, 'No, Messerschmitt better.' What the commander did after that is not reported!

Later that evening, Winston Churchill broadcast to the nation:

> The gratitude of every home in our island, in our Empire, and indeed throughout the world, except in the abodes of the guilty, goes out to the British airmen who, undaunted by odds, are turning the tides of the world war by their prowess and by their devotion. Never in the field of human conflict was so much owed by so many to so few.

In the days following, with the weather turning distinctly autumnal, the ferocity of the attacks was not so intense. Monday, 20th August saw several waves of enemy aircraft over Kent in the afternoon. The balloon barrage over Dover was once again attacked, together with further raids on Eastchurch, Manston and West Malling.

Manston, still recovering from previous raids, saw another raid three days later and was by now a shambles, with many personnel moved off the site. Sqd Ldr W. Grout, then a Sergeant, experienced one of the worst raids as he recounted in *Shellfire Memories* by D. Collyer:

> On the night of 23rd August I had been on defence duty at Thorn Farm, Pegwell Bay. When relieved at 6 am on the 24th, I returned to camp, had a clean up, shave and breakfast and then went to my office. I went to see the MO at the sick bay and asked for some tablets to keep me awake but he immediately ordered me to take 24 hours 'excused duty' and get some sleep. Approximately 30 to 40 minutes later, however, about 20 Ju88s attacked and one of the first bombs dropped on Hut B4, my hut! I was extremely lucky inasmuch as the blast blew the heavy door of my hut across the bed and I was buried underneath the debris. I eventually managed to dig myself out and assisted the casualties policemen in the roadway alongside the billets when three Me 109s screamed down out of the sun, with guns blazing. I dived headlong into a space between two walls forming the entrance to one of the huts, followed by two policemen who practically squashed me alive.
>
> I can also recall meeting the Station Chaplain, Sqd Ldr King, and accompanied him to the main shelter beneath the old parade square. This was full of airmen, not assigned to any specific duties. They were quite cheerful and morale was high – they were singing, arguing and playing cards. The Padre spoke to them and, as he was doing so, the NAAFI manageress came running in to us to say that she could not find any of her girls in the building. We found them safe and well in the beer cellar! Later that evening, I moved my staff records, etc. by lorry under cover of darkness down to an empty house at Westgate where I was given charge of a Standard van. The following day I was able to use it to get ample rations from the army catering depot at Dreamland in Margate. I returned to Manston to find it practically derelict and evacuated. Some of the squadron personnel were even camping out in the woods at Quex Park. How on earth Manston ever managed to continue is a wonder but continue it did.

This was also the day that the Polish Air Force had its first success over Britain, when a pilot from No 302 (Poznanski) Squadron shot down a Ju 88. From this day

Pilot Officer Keith Gillman of No 32 Squadron, Hawkinge, epitomised the spirit and courage of the British fighter pilot. He failed to return from a channel sortie on 25th August 1940, the first pilot from 32 Squadron to be lost in the Battle of Britain. (ATB)

on these intrepid warriors were to go from strength to strength, such was their hatred of the enemy that overran their homeland.

The *Daily Telegraph* of Tuesday, 27th August ran the headline: 'London's longest raid warning – enemy resorts to nuisance tactics. 46 Nazis shot down yesterday'. It was a long air-raid warning lasting six hours and although not known at the time, was an indication that tactics used by the Luftwaffe were changing in favour of hitting the capital cities of the country instead of the airfields.

This period also sounded the death knell for the Ju 87 Stuka. Against the modern RAF fighters, it was a slow and cumbersome aircraft which stood little chance of survival and was shot down in great numbers. Once an aircraft in which Goering had placed great faith, it was not to be seen again over England.

Time was running out if *Operation Sealion*, the invasion of England, was to take place. The impending change in weather would not allow a sea crossing of the Channel and Goering knew that the RAF was far from being cleared from the skies. The relentless bombing of airfields and towns was to enter a new and more powerful phase which would bring the RAF the closest yet to defeat. It began with another devastating attack on Biggin Hill.

> I wish to thank and congratulate all ranks, RAF and WAAF, for the spirit and calm courage and fortitude shown whilst our station was under heavy bombardment by the enemy, also for the fine display of initiative shown by all for getting the runways and station serviceable once again.

So spoke the CO, Gp Cpt R. Grice, on Friday, 30th August. A cloud layer over the Channel early that morning had deterred the Luftwaffe from making further attacks inland although assaults were made on shipping travelling through the Straits. The cloud persisted for several hours making the Observer Corps' job difficult. However, by noon, a build-up was detected on the radar and with a sudden lift of this cloud, coastal observers reported a wave of enemy aircraft crossing the coast. Whilst the main force made for the Surrey airfields, part of the force headed once again for Biggin Hill.

Back on the French coast the long-range guns were busy shelling Dover and Folkestone. The first that residents knew of a shell coming was a 'whooshing' sound followed by the explosion. Even though the flashes of the guns being fired could be seen on a clear day from the cliffs at Dover and Folkestone, the arrival of the big shells wrought havoc among the civilians, as one Dover resident reported:

> The first we knew of this shelling was when you could see a house collapse

No 165 Squadron airborne from Gravesend, 1940. (IWM)

without warning. There was no time for the ARP wardens to get people out of their houses and many perished without knowing what hit them. This was a nasty way to conduct war but later on we did the same when two heavy rail guns named Winnie and Pooh were sited just behind St Margaret's Bay. These were 14" naval guns, with a barrel weighing nearly 97 tons and with a 20-ton balance weight. In early August Mr Churchill arrived to see his namesake placed in position. The first day that Winnie fired shells at France was on 22nd August. Reports later stated that the shells had fallen within 300 yards of a German battery in Calais. We were now giving them as good as we got.

Friday, 30th August was also the day chosen by Mr Churchill to visit the ramparts of Dover Castle and look across the Channel to France. As he did so, newly-arrived No 79 Squadron from Biggin Hill swept overhead and despatched two German E-boats to the bottom of the sea. Arriving back at their new base the pilots encountered an atmosphere of apprehension and foreboding. After three attacks the station looked a pitiful sight with buildings bombed and red flags indicating where unexploded bombs lay. No sooner had they landed than the sirens began to wail.

Shortly before noon on this fateful Friday, 150 bombers escorted by a similar number of fighters swept in towards the airfield. For some reason many bombs fell outside the perimeter but several bombs did hit their targets. Detling and Eastchurch were subjected to similar attacks but again, these were not fighter airfields. At 6 pm that evening the enemy returned to Biggin Hill and carried out what was one of the worst attacks yet.

It was the time when most airmen and women were going into supper. The sound of approaching aircraft made them look up and then run for cover. No sirens had given a warning and the airfield was completely caught unawares. Six of No 79 Squadron's aircraft managed to get airborne and claimed two probables before the enemy aircraft reached the perimeter. However, those remaining certainly found their targets.

The crew of a Heinkel 111 enjoying the hot summer of 1940. (MAP)

The Battle Begins

Workshops, NAAFI, cookhouses, the sergeants' mess and airmen's quarters were all destroyed. One hangar was completely blown-up, two aircraft were destroyed and most of the station transport hit. A trench used by the WAAF received a direct hit. The doors of the shelter were blown in followed by the collapse of the walls. All the women were buried under the rubble, the cries and screams of those inside audible for some distance. All electricity, water and gas supplies were ruptured, with the smell of the latter causing vomiting. Some of the operation room staff defied the order to take cover and rushed to the roof to blaze away at the intruders with a Lewis gun, sadly to very little effect. Within minutes, however, the raiders had gone and almost in defiance but far too late, the sirens began to wail.

As rescuers rushed to the WAAF trench to help clear the rubble, the uncontrollable sound of sobbing could be heard. Working with bare hands, the men and women pulled away the bricks and tortured earth to discover one WAAF dead and many seriously injured. Someone could be heard reciting the *Lord's Prayer* as the padre arrived to bring some comfort and reassurance to the injured. Section Officer Felicity Hanbury worried about her girls. She saw all the injured packed off to hospital by ambulance before turning to clearing rubble. She wept uncontrollably as the full force of the horror came to her. After all the noise, though, the airfield seemed quiet and peaceful for it was indeed a lovely summer's evening.

Another victim was an airmen's shelter which, though meant to protect them, had disappeared under one high explosive bomb which landed nearby. Again, although the rescuers were quickly on the scene once the enemy aircraft had left, including some local miners with lamp lights, most of the men were found to be dead. As the bodies were carried out one by one, blankets were rushed to the scene to cover them. Some 40 airmen were to lie there waiting for the mortuary van to arrive. It was the duty of Gp Cpt R. Grice that night to write to all the relatives of the dead. Later that week a mass funeral was held, with relatives having travelled all through the night and from vast distances to be present. Many were crying as the padre conducted the service. Halfway through, the sound of sirens wailing close by was heard but no one moved to safety, such was the determination to see the dead receive a full Christian burial.

Meanwhile, the local post office engineers arrived to make sure Biggin Hill was back on air and with the aid of a temporary lash-up, the next morning saw the sector station back in action.

The dawn of 31st August heralded the promise of another fine and sunny day. On the airfields, it also brought a flurry of activity as ground crews prepared the aircraft for another day of combat. At Biggin Hill, Gravesend, Lympne and Hawkinge, crews were re-arming and re-fuelling the Hurricanes and Spitfires.

The WAAFs arrive at Biggin Hill. Far left is Sgt Helen Turner and second from right, Sgt Joan Mortimer. (RAF Biggin Hill)

*Sgt Helen Turner who remained at her switchboard throughout a raid until a colleague
threw her under a table. She was one of the three WAAFs awarded the MM.
(RAF Biggin Hill)*

The three WAAFs of Biggin Hill who were awarded the Military Medal during the Battle of Britain: R to L – Helen Turner, Elspeth Henderson and Joan Mortimer. (IWM)

Noon saw the enemy back at Biggin Hill where, once again, many bombs fell wide of their mark, although others hit the airfield. By 6 pm they were back, this time being well on the mark. The remaining buildings standing were demolished and the runways plastered. With a similar operations room construction to that of Detling, the duty controller ordered non-essential personnel to leave. Some refused to go, including WAAF Sgt Helen Turner. She remained at her switchboard just outside the operations room nerve centre. Suddenly a bomb landed nearby and severed most of the communications and electricity cables. Despite this, she feverishly worked to regain control and contact with Stanmore and the rest of the station. As she was still attempting to do so, an NCO rushed in and grabbed her from her seat just as a 500-pounder plunged through the roof. Fragments of bomb casing tore through Sgt Turner's equipment where seconds earlier she had been sitting. Close by, Cpl Elspeth Henderson of the WAAF was manning her switchboard to group headquarters. Splinters of glass and shrapnel were now flying around her switchboard and she decided it was time to drop to the floor. Still speaking into her headset and attempting to contact group, it was just in time as her console disappeared before her eyes. Later in the year both Elspeth Henderson and Helen Turner were to receive the Military Medal from the King for their bravery.

The next day, despite being a Sunday, offered no respite from the enemy. For the Luftwaffe and one pilot in particular, it was to be a disappointing day and one that would in no way see the defeat of the RAF. Flying with JG54 was one of the bright boys of the Luftwaffe, Lt Hellmuth Ostermann. He had been operational since the day war began. Like his British counterparts he was tired and in an interview for the book *Luftwaffe War Diaries* by Cajus Bekker, he gave his feelings about the war:

> Utter exhaustion from the English operations had begun to set in. For the first time one heard pilots talk of the prospects of a posting to a quieter sector. Day after day our unit had provided either escort for the bombers or flown fighter sweeps over the Channel as far as London. On one occasion I lost contact with my squadron. The whole Gruppe had split into dogfights and one hardly saw two planes together. The Spitfires showed themselves wonderfully manoeuvrable. Their aerobatics display, looping and rolling, opening fire in a climbing roll filled us with amazement and envy. There was a lot of shooting but not many hits.

He then went on to remember his first victory:

> At last I spotted a Spitfire on the tail of one of my comrades. I at once flung my machine around and went down after it. Now I was about 200 yards behind the Tommy. Steady does it – wait. The range was much too far. I crept slowly nearer till I was only a hundred yards away and the Spit's wings filled my reflector sight. Suddenly the Tommy opened fire and the Me in front of him went into a dive. I too had pressed the firing button after previously aiming carefully. I was only in a gentle glide as I did so. The Spit at once caught fire and with a long grey plume of smoke dived down vertically into the sea. This was my first victory and it felt good. I only hope the pilot baled out in time.

And so August ended on much the same note as it began. Sadly, it also ended on the day that saw Fighter Command's heaviest losses, with 39 fighters shot down and 14 pilots killed. Although no consolation, the Germans lost 41 aircraft over the 24-hour period. By dusk on the 31st the sky was full of vapour trails from previous conflicts, with every airfield in 11 Group looking ravaged and damaged. Biggin Hill, with its motto 'The Strongest Link', had received five raids in 48 hours. Manston was barely serviceable, whilst Hawkinge, Gravesend and Lympne were all mutilated.

Living near the airfields was a hazard, as Ronald F. Blay, with a home next to Manston recalled:

A graveyard of crashed British and German aircraft at No 86 Maintenance Unit.
(G. Ankorn)

Very soon after moving near to Manston, German planes with big black crosses would come over bombing and machine-gunning everything they could. One night we were on the way to the tunnel shelter (this was an old train tunnel fitted with many cubicles and bunks) carrying all our bedding when a German plane came over with his guns blazing, tearing slates off the houses nearby. We flung ourselves in a shop doorway and were terrified.

My brother and I would stand in the street after the air raids had finished and wave to the Spitfires and Hurricanes that were based at Manston. We watched a Messerschmitt fighter, all afire and glowing red hot, just miss our house. It crashed 100 yards away into the back of a hotel on the cliff top. The engine flew across the road and was caught on some railings where it hung on fire. About 50 yards away the RAF were filling a large petrol tank dug into the ground and they had to move fast for fear of it exploding. Whilst it was exciting living near an airfield, it was also very dangerous!

Yet, still the long, hot summer continued, as Kent became referred to as 'Hell's Corner'. As August turned to September, Mr Churchill in a wireless broadcast stated: 'We must prepare for heavier fighting in the month of September. The need of the enemy to obtain a decision is very great. The whole nation will take its example from our airmen and will be proud to share part of the dangers with them.'

Whilst the barges still remained in the French ports, the threat of invasion was still imminent. Even so, Goering's objective of clearing the skies of the RAF had not been met. Angry and disillusioned, he called his top unit commanders together for a conference. When he asked Werner Molders what were his requirements for his squadron in order to finish off the RAF, the answer was: 'More powerful engines.' Turning to Adolf Galland, Goering asked the same question. Galland answered, 'I should like an outfit of Spitfires for my group, Herr Reichsmarschall'. Such an answer made Goering speechless and he stamped off, growling as he went.

For Hell's Corner, the next month was to be a decisive one.

Chapter 6

Fighting for our Lives

September to October 1940

The **first anniversary** of the declaration of war against Germany was to coincide with a change in German policy. Hitler, outraged by the fact that bombs had been dropped on Berlin, told Goering to 'exterminate British cities'. In a major speech at the Sportspalast in Berlin on 4th September, he said:

> When the British Air Force drops two or three or four thousand kilograms of bombs, then we will drop in one night 150, 250, 300 or 400 thousand kilograms. In England they're filled with curiosity and keep asking 'Why doesn't he come?' Be calm, he's coming. He's coming.

Though not known at the time, this was to be a strategic turning point in the air war as the heat of battle was to be slowly turned away from the destruction of the airfields and taken to the major cities, London in particular. With this change in policy, Hitler still believed that an invasion was possible if the morale of the civilian population were to be brought down. But the civilian population had no intention of giving in.

In all Kent's cities and towns, as far as possible, life carried on as normal. It was the hop-picking season and many travelled from the East End of London to join the locals in the hop gardens. They were not to be deprived of their working holidays, as they arrived on trains at Paddock Wood, Headcorn, Tenterden and many other

The East Enders still enjoyed their annual holiday during 1940. (Kent Messenger)

country stations. Carrying their few belongings to the huts that the farmer provided, one elderly lady from the East End commented, 'We're not afraid of Jerry – damned if we are.' Such was the feeling in Kent in September 1940, a month that was to see attacks on civilians, as well as the military. A month in which the long hot summer was to continue and a month in which the spirit of the county did not diminish. Never before was the county motto, 'Unconquered', more apt.

From the book *Hell's Corner 1940* by H.R.P. Boorman, came just one indication of that indomitable spirit:

> At Hawkinge aerodrome a Sgt pilot who had been awarded a DFM and bar and with 14 enemy kills to his credit, always flew the same aeroplane, a Hurricane, which he considered his own. During one of the many raids that the airfield received, his Hurricane was hit and damaged beyond repair on the ground. He was furious and saw red. He rushed over to the first available aircraft which was ticking over and took off in chase of the

bombers. Catching up with them as they streaked for home, he shot one of them down in revenge for his own aircraft. Only upon landing back at Hawkinge did he realise that he had taken the CO's aircraft! In his own words, 'That was just one more of the b-------s down.'

The new month began badly for one place in Kent – Maidstone, the county town. It had enjoyed a relatively quiet few months compared to other towns in the county but this was to change on Thursday, 5th September when, once again, the main targets were in the south-east corner.

From Dover, the French coast was clearly visible once an early morning mist had cleared. At the headquarters of Luftflotte 2 in Brussels, Generalfeldmarschall Albert Kesselring was worrying about his confrontation the previous week with his commander, Goering. His instructions from Goering were plain and simple: hit the British in any way possible in order for the invasion to commence. Down the chain of command, Major Martin Mettig, the enigmatic leader of JG54, was issuing his

Vapour trails over St Francis' church, Maidstone – evidence of heavy dog fighting.
(Kent Messenger -ref. 3783/1)

orders of battle. The first Gruppe based at Guines was to conduct a sortie over Kent as part of two major attacks to be launched simultaneously in the morning. With an early morning call, the pilots were in the air and formatting upon the bombers by 9 am. The Me 109s of JG54 were to escort some 30 bombers heading for the airfields of Croydon, Biggin Hill and Eastchurch.

Fourteen RAF squadrons were also airborne at around the same time to intercept and break up the enemy armada which, by 9.45 am, had crossed the coast at Dungeness. One of the squadrons tasked with this was No 19 Squadron, based at Duxford but that morning flying from the satellite airfield at Fowlmere. Led by Sqd Ldr P.C. Pinkham, their orders were to patrol an area from Hornchurch in Essex to the River Thames.

Down below, the people of Maidstone were going about their business unaware of the drama about to unfold. The hop-picking season was well under way with

'We are not giving up our holidays for anyone.' Kent hop pickers defy the enemy, 1940.
(Kent Messenger -ref. 34/714/25/89)

One that came down in a hop garden at Horsmonden in 1940, guarded by the RAF and watched by curious pickers (even babes in arms). (Kent Messenger -ref. PD1456671)

every hop garden, of which there were many, filled with enthusiastic pickers. Never daunted by the sight or sound of the enemy, they watched as the enemy aircraft flew overhead on their way to a target.

In the sky above, Sgt B.J. Jennings sighted the enemy formation and identified them as Do 215s at around 15,000 ft. Looking up further he saw an escort of Me 109s and 110s in a vic formation 5,000 ft above. Sqd Ldr Pinkham then called 'A' flight to attack the fighters and 'B' flight, the bombers. Wheeling his aircraft round, the leader of Green section, FO L.A. Haines was flying Spitfire X4059 He gave a vivid account later of his conflict with one particular Me 109, part of the bomber escort, that was to bring destruction to the county town:

> Whilst leading Green section on a patrol over Chatham, numerous enemy aircraft were sighted at approximately 10.05 hrs. Enemy formation consisted of unidentified bombers, Me 110 and Me 109 fighters heading south-west. Line action was ordered and whilst following Blue leader into the enemy

A dramatic photo of a Spitfire closing in for the kill.

formation, I was attacked by two Me 109 fighters. I did a steep turn and as they dived past me I opened my engine and chased after the second one. I waited until I was at 200 yards' range and opened fire. After a five-second burst the enemy aircraft's engine began issuing puffs of smoke and the pilot began hedge-hopping. I kept in range and let him have the rest of my ammunition when I noticed a burst of flame from the engine. It also issued a continuous stream of black smoke. He was then over the fields and approaching Maidstone. On reaching more or less the centre of the town he climbed his aircraft to around 800 ft and baled out. The enemy aircraft crashed in flames in the garden of a house and the pilot landed safely. The aircraft was camouflaged in the usual way and the pilot tried various weaving tactics to shake me off his tail.

In another report regarding the same incident it appears as though the Me 109 fell victim to another hit from a Hurricane of No 46 (F) Squadron, flying from Stapleford Tawney, the satellite airfield to North Weald in Essex. Fl Lt A.C. Rabagliati filed this report upon landing:

> I sighted a large formation of enemy aircraft five miles south of Sheppey at approximately 5,000 ft above. I climbed to 12,000 ft and spotted a 109 on the tail of a Spitfire (FO Haines' aircraft). Gave this enemy a three second burst and he blew up resulting in a flash and explosion in the enemy's port wing root. He took no evasive action and did not appear to have seen me as the aircraft went into a steep dive and according to my number two and three, hit the ground in Maidstone in or near the town jail. I estimate that I fired about 60 rounds at this aircraft.

Few witnessed the final dramatic moments of the Me 109, as most were taking refuge in cellars or shelters. It crashed into the rear of No 6 Hardy Street, Maidstone, tearing off the gable of one room and finally embedding itself into the lawn with a large explosion. Mrs Gladys Hattersley was taking refuge in the cellar with her son Derrick, aged three months, and sister-in-law Mrs K. Thompsett and her son.

Within a short time, an Auxiliary Fire Service trailer pump crew arrived from their station in Hope Street. Section Officer Cecil Diplock immediately attempted to extinguish the fire, made more difficult due to ammunition exploding all over the place. Several ARP wardens were now on the scene and managed to get the occupants out of the damaged house through the front cellar window. Slowly the aircraft burnt itself out and, as it did so, the temptation to obtain a trophy became too much for the fire crew. They managed to cut the Swastika from the tail using their axes but were later forced to hand it over to the police. An army unit arrived to guard what was left of the 109 lest further souvenir hunters arrived on the scene.

The pilot, Unteroffizier Fritz Hotzelmann, had descended by parachute and after hitting the roof of a house, landed safely in the road breaking both legs in the process. Dr Henry Cotton of No 1 Mobile Medical Unit arrived and administered first aid after which Hotzelmann was taken to the West Kent hospital in Maidstone under an armed escort.

One of the first men on the scene was Bill Holland, a driver with an air raid precautions first aid team. He recalled seeing the pilot fall into the road.

> I ran towards him and released his parachute harness. He was wearing a blue/grey tunic and trousers with flashings of yellow around the collar. The trouser bottoms were tucked into his flying boots, his face was covered in blood and he was semi-conscious. He held up his hand, I suppose in surrender, as I helped him as best I could. In return the army gave me part of his parachute as a souvenir.

The incident brought many sightseers despite the sirens constantly wailing. Unteroffizier Hotzelmann spent a short time in a military hospital before being transferred to a POW camp in the north of England and then on to Canada. Many years later a local historian, Tony Webb, from whom this account came, corresponded with Fritz Hotzelmann who sent him a graphic account of the aerial battle. On that fateful day he was flying with his No 2 when he saw a squadron of Spitfires in the sun. Alerting the rest of the squadron, he dived on to some Spitfires below them. He blacked out for several seconds and when he came to he saw a Spitfire firing at him and found bullets hitting his cooling system. Further bursts hit the engine, resulting in Fritz being forced to bale out. Many years later the crash site was excavated by the Kent Battle of Britain Museum which recovered several parts of the Me 109.

Unteroffizier Hotzelmann – crashed Maidstone 5th September 1940 but survived.
(A. Webb Collection)

Von Werra's crashed Me 109 at Marden, Kent, 5th September 1940.
(Kent Messenger -ref. 3113/2)

> I am not at all happy to bee her and I hop to see Jou agam but not as prisonner of war but as a friend.
>
> F. Ohlwra
>
> German luftwaffe
>
> 5 of September is the second year of war.

Letter written by von Werra shortly after his capture.

Another victim that day was Oberleutnant Baron Franz von Werra and his Me 109E-4. He was shot down during a diversionary sweep and force-landed at Winchet Hill, Love's Farm, Marden. Captured unhurt, his life as a POW and his many escapes were related in the book *The One That Got Away* by Kendal Burt and James Leasor. It was later made into a film featuring Hardy Kruger as von Werra.

As the hot September continued, there began a noticeable change in the Luftwaffe tactics. Still the RAF had not been cleared from the skies, yet Kesselring and his commanders were still crossing off airfields as out of

Franz von Werra pictured in 1944

action and overestimating Fighter Command casualties. Between 24th August and 6th September, the command had lost 295 Hurricanes and Spitfires, with another 171 badly damaged. Reserves from the other groups, however, had allowed these losses to be replenished, unknown to the enemy. The production of fighters was going from strength to strength although the loss of pilots was still a worrying feature for Dowding.

What was considered the fourth phase of the battle began on 7th September. Still the timetable for the invasion of England was not going to schedule due to the resistance of the RAF. The change of policy by the German high command mentioned earlier was now to take effect as raids on the airfields became fewer and the main target became London. Whilst this was good news for Dowding and Fighter Command, it was bad news for the civilian population. The Blitz proper had begun.

With so many enemy aircraft now crossing Kent to bomb London, even more conflicts were taking place over the county. Saturday, 7th September saw several heavy attacks on the capital, with many enemy aircraft falling to the guns of Fighter Command, as well as to the ack-ack guns. At Biggin Hill No 92 Squadron had flown in from Pembrey whilst No 501 were still at Gravesend. At the radar stations on the coast, the early watch waited for the telltale signs of a big build-up over France. They were late coming that morning. In fact, it was not until mid afternoon when the blips appeared on the cathode tubes.

Soon the stations were reporting several waves of enemy aircraft to the Stanmore filter room as they crossed the Channel and made for Hawkinge. It was a severe blow to this forward airfield as bombs straddled the officers' mess, one of the remaining hangars, the station headquarters and an army defence post, the latter killing one soldier and injuring a further dozen. Bombs also landed in the village of Hawkinge where an air raid shelter was struck, sadly killing five people. As late afternoon approached the radar stations began to see huge formations lining up. These were the first of many armadas coming to attack London and the civilian population. From bases in France, Holland and Belgium, they attacked the capital leaving raging fires around Dockland. In a war broadcast Robin Duff, a BBC correspondent, watched the City of London burn:

> St Paul's cathedral was the pivot of the main attack. All around the flames were leaping up into the sky. There the cathedral stood, magnificently firm, untouched in the centre of all this destruction. As I walked along the street it was almost impossible to believe that these fires could be subdued. I was walking between solid walls of fire. Houses and office buildings had fallen

down with a roaring crash. Panes of glass were cracking everywhere and every street was criss-crossed with fire hoses. Men were fighting the fires from the top of 100 ft ladders, others were pushing their way into burning buildings. I wondered if London could survive such an onslaught.

The next morning, people woke to the news that 306 civilians had been killed and 1,337 seriously injured. This was the first mass daylight raid on the capital. Further attacks would be made at night as well as by day.

Although the attacks of the 7th September were devastating for the capital, many enemy aircraft did not return home. One destined not to return that fine afternoon was the Me 109E (s/n 5798) of Unterofficier Werner Goetting, an aircraft of the 1st Staffel of Lehrgeschwader 2 operating from Calais-Marke airfield. It was late afternoon before Werner Goetting was scrambled on his 123rd mission. He carried a 250 kg bomb underneath his fuselage and was carrying out what was termed a 'free chase mission'. Crossing the Kent coast he was attacked over Canterbury at 5.30 pm by

Re-arming a Spitfire at Gravesend. (IWM)

the Hurricane of Sgt Furst, a pilot flying with No 310 (Czech) Squadron operating from Duxford. After a chase lasting several minutes in which Sgt Furst managed to out-turn his opponent, he had the satisfaction of seeing his bullets hit the 109. Suddenly, flames could be seen coming from the Daimler Benz engine and Werner Goetting realised he had to get out. Leaving his diving aircraft successfully, his parachute opened and he landed near the Little Stour River at Wickhambreux, near Canterbury.

His arrival and subsequent capture were witnessed by a local farmer, Mr W. Williams, who later gave his story to the *Kent Messenger* and in a letter in 1977 to Maidstone historian Tony Webb:

> I had a farm at Stourmouth near Canterbury being roughly three miles from Wickhambreux. It was one beautiful day in mid September, the height of the Battle of Britain, the time being around 5 pm in the afternoon, when the pilot of the shot down plane landed in our village behind the church. I was standing in the yard of my farm when I saw him drifting towards my orchard. I could see him pulling the cords on his parachute to try to land away from the trees. This he was able to do and landed on the other side of the church. The first person to encounter him was the vicar, the Reverend Whitehouse, joined later by myself. However, within a few minutes, a large number of people had arrived. We took him into the rectory close by and our local St John ambulance man attended to a bullet wound on the left-hand side of his cheek. In the meantime, the vicar had supplied him with a clean shirt, etc., as he was covered in blood. By now the army had arrived to take him away to be interrogated. One feature of interest to us all was that the pilot of the Hurricane that had shot him down circled around him until he saw that he had been spotted on landing. He then flew very low over us and gave the thumbs-up sign before flying away. Perhaps after all chivalry was not dead. I remember that in the pocket of the German pilot was a recent ticket to the Berlin Opera House. If ever he comes back to the country I would be pleased to show him where he first set foot on British soil.

Thirty-seven years later, in 1977 Werner Goetting did return to Wickhambreux where he was presented with a painting of himself. He had come over from Germany to see the excavation of his Me 109 by the Kent Battle of Britain Museum. Many parts of his aircraft were recovered and he related, in very good English, his account of the day he did not return home:

> I looked to my left and saw a plane passing by. I pulled the stick to get

Werner Goetting (right) and Geoff Stephens at the crash site in 1977.
(via A. Webb Collection)

away and climbed sharply but he must have turned and come for me from behind because the bullets started shattering my canopy and hitting the instrument panel. The steering was hit and I could not control my plane so I had to bale out. I thought it was the end.

What he also remembered was that the vicar and his wife looked after him and tended his wounds, together with the ambulance man. They also gave him a cup of tea and a new shirt: 'They were very kind to me indeed. At first I was a little nervous at coming back all these years after but also a little excited. Everyone has been so kind to me and very friendly.'

Over the next few days, most raids were directed at London and the major cities, and were carried out from mid afternoon onwards leaving the mornings relatively quiet. On 13th September, when Hitler gathered together his chiefs of staff, he was informed that British opposition was weak and the German casualty rate low. This was false information and gave the impression to Hitler that the time was rapidly

Messerschmitt Me 110 crashed at Lenham on 11th September 1940: Fw Brinkman and Uffz Kruespho were captured and taken prisoner. (Kent Messenger -ref. 3786/3)

approaching when he could give the decision to launch *Operation Sealion*. He accordingly timed it for 17th September when he was assured that five days of good weather would allow the Luftwaffe to entirely clear the skies of the RAF.

Sunday, 15th September dawned misty, which heralded the promise of another fine day in this continuing hot summer. Now celebrated as Battle of Britain Day, it was remarkable for its complete, not partial, change of German policy in hitting at the civilian population. Plans had been made for one decisive blow that would finish the RAF and allow 'Sealion' to proceed. At 11 am mass formations were seen building up over Calais and Boulogne. No 11 Group put up eleven squadrons to patrol the skies from Essex to Hampshire as the enemy formations approached. At Biggin Hill, the first call for the pilots of No 92 Squadron came at 4 am. Dressing quickly they moved to the dispersal huts to await a scramble. Sitting in armchairs some dozed, others read, or nervously awaited the jangling of the telephone.

That morning at the headquarters of 11 Group, the Prime Minister and Mrs

Churchill stood in the operations room, deep underground, watching Air Vice Marshal Park and his commanders direct the forthcoming battle. Seeing all the 'squadrons airborne' lights come on, Mr Churchill asked, 'What reserves have we?' The answer was, 'None, Sir.'

No 92 Squadron were scrambled at 11.03 am: 'Squadron patrol Maidstone – Angels 20 – Rendevous with 72 Squadron over base.' The quiet voice of the controller was drowned in a rush of feet as the pilots grabbed their helmets and goggles and ran to the waiting aircraft. Over the coast the bombers and their escorts were droning on. Flying with the escort in a Me 109 that day was Professor Hassel von Wedel, now the Luftwaffe historian. Over Maidstone the enemy were attacked by several Hurricanes from as far away as Coltishall in Norfolk. Von Wedel was one of the first to be hit and, with his cooling system gone, he coaxed his engine to continue as he headed for a field with several buildings. It turned out to be Hans Farm on Romney Marsh. As he crash-landed, the local ARP were quickly on the scene and a report was sent to Maidstone at 12.30 pm: 'German aircraft crashed at Hans Farm, Bilsington. Pilot taken prisoner. One child killed, 1 or 2 people injured, 1 suffering from shock. Three farm sheds extensively damaged – 1 small car completely wrecked.'

Whilst this was an apt description of what happened, the reality was considerably more terrible. The farm was owned by Mr W. Daw, who was about to take a drive with his wife and daughter who were waiting for him in the car that was garaged in one of the outbuildings. Mr Daw saw the 109 crash land and not stop but continued to head for those very sheds. Being unable to do anything he stood rooted to the spot as the 109 smashed into the building and the car. Sadly, Mrs Daw and her daughter were killed outright and the car was unrecognisable. As the dazed von Wedel climbed out of the cockpit, which was still virtually intact, and saw what had happened he broke down, crying uncontrollably and attempting to apologise to Mr Daw. He was eventually led away to the local police station before being sent to a POW camp. He was later killed in a Russian attack on Berlin in 1945.

The afternoon saw further raids, with another incident happening within the vicinity of Maidstone. Included in these attacks were the He IIIs of Kampfgeschwader 53 operating from Lille-Nord. One particular aircraft, 6843 code A1-GM and flown by Oberfeldwebel Schmittborn, carried an extra passenger in the form of Major Max Gruber, the commander of the 2nd Gruppe, who had decided to join them on a raid to the Victoria Docks and oil storage installations on the River Thames.

Approaching south of the Thames at 23,000 ft, they came under intense fire from the anti-aircraft guns along their route. One hit set the starboard engine on fire and, struggling to keep airborne, Oberfeldwebel Schmittborn turned away from the main formation, losing height as he did so. Although attacked further by several Hurricanes and Spitfires, the German crew manning the guns successfully managed to keep further attacks at bay although a bullet from one of the attacking fighters hit and killed one gunner. Now down to a dangerous level, Schmittborn shouted to the crew to brace themselves for a landing.

Ahead lay Burgess Farm at Frittenden where hop picking was in full swing. Unable to hold the aircraft any longer, it crashed down among the bines in a wheels-up landing. Poles and hops flew everywhere but it was not the area in which the hop pickers were busy stripping the bines. As the tail section broke away the aircraft came to a rest and the crew scrambled out. It was none too soon as the aircraft burst into flames. Seeing the large black column of smoke ascending skywards and hearing the crash, the pickers ran towards the area and saw the crew wandering around in a daze. But for the intervention of army men who were stationed nearby, the hop pickers would have lynched the crew. Those with minor injuries were sent to Benenden cottage hospital whilst the rest were held in the cellar of a local house, watched over by the Home Guard. The following morning they were all transferred to an interrogation centre. At the nearby Bell Inn, the landlord's daughter was home on leave from the ATS. She visited the crash site and acquired one of the aircraft's propeller blades as a war trophy for display in her father's pub. It remained there for the rest of the war before being transferred to Frittenden village hall.

The next morning the *Daily Telegraph* ran one of its boldest headlines yet: '175 RAIDERS DOWN – ONE IN TWO DESTROYED – RAF LOSE 30'. And what mattered above all else was that within 48 hours, Hitler issued the signal which indefinitely postponed the invasion of Britain.

The rest of September saw raids on Dowding's airfields dwindle as the ferocity of the Luftwaffe turned to London and other major cities. This did mean, however, that large armadas of enemy aircraft were crossing the county, some dropping their bombs at random and making life for people very dangerous.

With the increase in night raids on the capital, Fighter Command was struggling to cope with shooting down enemy aircraft at night. One solution was the introduction of the Boulton Paul Defiant to a night fighter role. The Defiant was one of the more maligned aircraft of the battle. With no forward firing guns, all fire power was concentrated in a turret situated behind the pilot. This had proved successful in shooting down enemy aircraft earlier in the year but once the Germans learned to use the greater agility of their fighters to engage the Defiant head-on or from below, it was taken off front-line squadrons. The type was subsequently utilised as a night fighter, with one of its first successes in the role coming on the night of 17th September, once again over the county town, Maidstone.

That evening saw the bomber crews of the 3rd Staffel of KG54 being briefed for the night attacks. Amongst the pilots was Leutnant Rudolf Ganslmayr who would be flying a Ju 88A-1 (s/n 2152) to attack the London Docks. Later the same evening, ten aircraft of the 3rd Staffel took off from Evreux airfield at 10.21 pm, just ten out of a total of 268 enemy bombers that were to be deployed against London. At around 11.15 pm Leutnant Ganslmayr and his crew, now separated from the main formation, were to the south of Bexley and heading for the docks.

Also airborne that night was Defiant L6988 of No 141 Squadron out of Biggin Hill. The fighter was flown by Sgt G.L. Laurance, with Sgt W.T. Chard as the air gunner and was one of two from 'B' flight on patrol. Ordered to fly a line from Maidstone to Tonbridge at 15,000 ft, Sgt Laurance saw an enemy aircraft silhouetted in the bright moonlight. He turned and gave chase, managing to overtake to allow Sgt Chard to bring his guns to bear upon the Ju 88. Just a short burst forced the enemy to jettison two large bombs before he made off at high speed with the Defiant in hot pursuit. Managing to get into another position to allow Sgt Chard to again fire and hit the bomber, both men had the satisfaction of seeing a fire take hold within the aircraft, which went into a steep dive, exploding as it went down.

'Fallen Eagle': destruction by night of Ltn Ganslmayr's Junkers 88 over Maidstone, 17th September 1940. An original oil painting by Ralph Bristow. (via A. Webb)

Fuselage of the Ju 88 brought down in Tonbridge Road, Maidstone, on the night of 17th September 1940, attacked by Defiant of 'B' flight, No 141 Squadron and the West Malling Airfield ack-ack battery. The crew are buried in Maidstone Cemetery.

The Ju 88 crashed in the St Andrew's Close area of Maidstone, spreading debris all around. The rear section of the fuselage fell in the front garden of Nos 410 and 412 Tonbridge Road whilst the tail section demolished a greenhouse backing onto Bellingham's Farm. At 11.40 pm, ARP wardens and Home Guard personnel rushed to the scene to quell the fires with stirrup pumps and sandbags. Not until 2.15 am were they brought under control. Due to the danger of unexploded bombs and to allow recovery work to begin, the area was evacuated. Three of the crew were found dead in the aircraft wreckage, whilst a fourth lay on the lawn to the rear of No 3 St Andrews Close. The body of a woman, Mrs J. Bridgeland, was also recovered from the gutted house. The final report of this one incident was recorded as:

> Fire at six houses; two reported gutted and badly damaged. Three houses damaged by fire also one garage plus one car. Eight other houses damaged with a school receiving a damaged roof. Four crew members dead plus one woman dead. One man and one woman slightly injured.

A temporary guard was mounted by the Royal West Kent Regiment until daylight when the wreckage was taken away to No 86 Maintenance Unit at Sundridge near Sevenoaks. The crew were buried with full military honours on Friday, 20th September at Maidstone borough cemetery. It had been just one incident in many that same night.

From mid-September, with the increase in night raids, the people of Kent suffered nights of disturbed sleep as the bombers headed for London. Many bombs were dropped at random, with several areas of the county affected by incendiaries and high explosive bombs. Sittingbourne had its first experience of the bombing on Sunday, 29th September. A lone raider dropped a couple of bombs in the Murston district before making off towards Doddington. He immediately returned, however, and a number of further bombs were dropped near Park Road, demolishing several shops and damaging dozens of others. There were eight deaths and numerous casualties. Thirty cars were destroyed in Pullens Garage but the prompt action of the fire service saved the petrol pumps.

Yet still the people of Kent tried to carry on as normal as possible. An East End regular hop picker recalled in *Wartime Kent* by Oonagh Hyndman:

> I remember one Sunday morning coming back from the local pub, the Red Cow. Ten men were walking along the lane talking and joking. Suddenly the siren sounded but we took no notice and continued walking. Just as we got to the farm, we saw the Germans coming over, swarms of them all in formation. Then we heard the bombs coming down so we quickly dived into the ditch alongside the lane. I stood up and saw a string of bombs go straight across the farm. We ran down to the hop pickers' huts where the women and children were. They were crying and screaming, huddled together in the huts, but thank God no one was hurt. The first bomb dropped in the orchard 50 yards away and the next one was in the hop field which was just beyond that. That was an unexploded bomb which had sliced through the soil like butter. My mate and I went over to look at it and only then did we realise that we could be blown to bits if it exploded now.

The families were evacuated from the huts and put up in a barn and some cowsheds. We finished picking the hops and tried to carry on as normal.

Friday, 27th September 1940 will be forever known as 'Black Friday' to many

An Me 109 dives to its doom on Sunday, 29th September 1940.
Note the resulting fireball.

people in mid-Kent. It was the day that bomb-carrying Me 110s, escorted by Me 109s, together with Heinkels, Dorniers and Junkers, dropped their bombs indiscriminately all over Kent. With London the intended target once again, the first sign of activity on the radar screens began at 8 am, just as the morning watch was taking over. What the operators were witnessing was the last of the big daytime assaults by large bomber formations. Henceforth, the night blitz would take over.

Nos 92 and 72 Squadrons were still at Biggin Hill, whilst No 66 Squadron with Spitfires was at Gravesend. Elsewhere in the neighbouring counties, the Hurricane and Spitfire squadrons, together with the three Kent squadrons, were ready to do battle, one beginning over Kent at just after 9 am. The fighters tore into the battle, ripping the German formations to pieces. From Sheppey to Dungeness, the sky was covered with vapour trails, evidence of hard dog fighting. In minutes the Germans were turning and attempting to flee back across the Channel. Once the skies were clear of the enemy, the fighters landed, refuelled, re-armed and were back in the air to meet the second wave at 11.45 am.

Once again the Germans were harried crossing Kent, with the result that many jettisoned their bombs and turned for home. Down below it was the job of the ARP to note where the bombs fell and the ones that did not explode on impact, known as 'UXBs' (unexploded bombs). It was then the job of the bomb disposal teams to deal with them. Two such incidents occurred in the county town, one with sad and deadly results.

Of the 42 bombs that fell upon Maidstone on Black Friday, twelve were delayed action or failed to explode. In Salem Street, a small cul-de-sac of eleven early Victorian properties, with outside toilets and a single cold-water tap, one bomb fell to the rear of the property failing to explode. No 11 Salem Street was the home of Frank Street, his wife and daughter who were in the house when the bomb fell. Showered with broken glass, they were forced to leave the house and be temporarily billeted with another family. The practice at this time of the war was that most UXBs were left for 168 hours before attempts were made to defuse them unless they were in vital locations. In the case of No 11, it was October before such an operation was carried out by No 6 Section of the Royal Engineers. However, during the controlled explosion the roof of the house was badly damaged, leaving Mr Street and his family homeless for some time until it was finally repaired.

The same raid saw a delayed action bomb drop through a bedroom and the floor of the Foresters Arms, a favourite watering hole for town people. Miraculously, no one was killed. Anne, an Irish maid, and the landlord's daughter, Patricia Marshall, sought refuge under a row of beer barrels, none of which exploded! On Thursday, 6th October, the Bomb Disposal Unit of the Royal Engineers arrived to render the

Bomb damage to the Foresters Arms public house in Maidstone, 27th September 1940.
The bomb dropped was not defused until 6th October.

250 kg bomb safe. Work progressed well until, at 1.30 pm, there was a searing flash and a deafening explosion. Within seconds, the Foresters Arms was a pile of rubble, sadly entombing two Sappers who had been assisting in the de-fuse. Desperately their colleagues dug through the rubble with bare hands, joined minutes later by the ARP officer, police and Maidstone fire brigade. It was too late, however, to save the two men and, later in the afternoon, the bodies of Lance Corporal Frederick James Appleton and Sapper James Alexander Orr were recovered from the debris.

For the county town, this was the worst raid experienced during the war. Further damage stretched from the south to the north of the borough. Two bombs landed in the museum gardens close to St Faith's church, making a huge crater. The explosion split the tower, with the long crack passing through the dial of the church clock. At the end of Black Friday, ten men, eleven women and a child lay dead. Twenty-two men and 22 women and a child were seriously injured, together with 20 men, 24 women and four children slightly injured. With the change in German tactics, this rapidly became a people's war.

Mr Churchill had said, 'The odds were great; our margins small; the stakes infinite.' This statement was most appropriate, for the last day of September gave a slight indication that the Battle of Britain was ebbing to its close. Despite this, however, many ferocious attacks took place over the county. The radar stations did not have to wait long before the WAAF plotters were speaking to the filter room, warning them of a large build-up over France.

Just one hour separated the first two major attacks. In the first wave came 30 bombers and 100 fighters. The second had 60 aircraft but crossing the coast at Dungeness, they were attacked by Fighter Command. On this occasion no aircraft reached London but again, many dropped their bombs over the Kent countryside. They were back again at midday when another fierce battle took place, followed by a lesser raid at 3.10 pm. Twenty minutes later a major force of over 100 aircraft crossed Kent and despite fierce opposition from the RAF and ack-ack gunners, 30 reached and bombed London. By dusk the county was littered with aircraft wreckage. With the day's battle over, 47 enemy aircraft were destroyed for a loss of 20 RAF fighters and with eight pilots killed or wounded.

What is now termed the fifth and final phase of the battle began on 1st October and finished on 31st October. On October 10, Sgt Allgood who had been posted to 253(F) Squadron at Kenley only twelve days before, took off from Kenley in Hurricane L1928, together with eight other Hurricanes. He was flying 'tail-end charlie'. Patrolling over Maidstone his Hurricane suddenly went into a steep dive with the engine screaming at maximum revs. Within seconds the aircraft had sliced through the roof of No. 63 Albion Place in Maidstone and had cut its way through

Nos.59 and 61, with the engine embedding itself in the cellars of both houses. The Hurricane burst into flames killing Sgt Allgood and two families of three women and five children. Among the civilian casualties were Mrs Doris Woods and her baby daughter of No. 61, together with her mother, Mrs Elizabeth Wooding, and four sisters and a brother who had been accommodated in No. 61 since their own home in nearby Astley Street had become severely damaged during an air raid on 2nd September. It was a month of more major attacks both on London and the airfields.

At Biggin Hill, a further raid did damage but did not put the station out of action. One reason for this was that the operations room, demolished in previous raids, had been moved to a requisitioned country house named Towerfields. Nos 92 and 72 Squadrons were still resident with No 66 Squadron at Gravesend, the latter shortly to move over to West Malling which was now ready to accept a resident squadron after the heavy attacks. Whilst it played no major part in the battle, West Malling was destined to become the premier nightfighter station in Fighter Command from 1941 onwards.

With London still the main target, the raging fires were clearly visible from Kent. In Goudhurst in the Weald of Kent, Gladys Townsend would stand and watch the red glow in the night sky as she recalled in an interview in 1990:

> You could see all the fires burning from my house. It was really remarkable and if it hadn't been wartime, it would have been wonderful to have been able to see that far. But that terrible red glow over London made my blood go cold. We always knew that London was to get it when all those black swarms of German aircraft flew over Kent. We did feel sorry for all those Londoners.

In mid October the long, hot summer began to change to a more autumnal feeling. Although cloud cover was increasing day by day, the huge formations continued to batter London and the major cities. For Dowding and his airfields, the relief from constant attack allowed Fighter Command to regain some strength although, even at this late stage of the battle, pilot numbers were still worrying.

Across the Channel it was the new mark of Spitfire that was causing the Luftwaffe a problem. Ulrich Steinhilper was a fighter pilot with JG52, which usually flew from Coquelles, now the site of the French side of the Channel Tunnel entry and exit. In a letter to his parents (quoted in *Spitfire On My Tail* by Ulrich Steinhilper and Peter Osbourne, Independent Books, 1990) he expressed the worry of the Luftwaffe:

> The British have a new engine in their Spitfires and our Messerschmitts can hardly keep up with it. We have also made improvements and had also

*Gravesend 1940 – No 66 Squadron in the clubhouse: Ft/Lt R. Oxspring,
Sqd Ldr R.H.A. Leigh (CO, seated), PO C.A.W. Bodie, Ft/Lt K.M. Gillies,
PO A.B. Watkinson, PO H.M.T. Hero, PO H.R. (Dizzy) Allen-Hewitt (Adjutant),
PO J.A. Hutton (Int. Officer), PO H. Reilly. (Kent Messenger)*

One of the few: Sgt Pilot Tim Frith, No 92 Squadron, Biggin Hill, killed 9th October 1940, aged 26. (ATB)

Bomb damage in Albion Place, Maidstone, where Sgt Augood crashed on 10th October 1940. The crash killed the pilot and two families of three women and five children. (Kent Messenger -ref. 3847/1)

some new engines but there is no more talk of absolute air superiority. The other day we tangled with these new Spitfires and had three losses against one success. I ended up against two Spitfires with all my guns jammed. There was no alternative but to get the hell out of it.

The new engine in the Spitfire was the Merlin XII, fitted with a two-stage supercharger. This gave the aircraft not only a better rate of climb and speed but also an improved service ceiling. Eight days after his letter to his parents, Oberleutnant Steinhilper was shot down by a Spitfire from No 74 Squadron, then commanded by legendary fighter ace 'Sailor' Malan and flying from Biggin Hill at 9.40 am. He had been part of an escort to another group of Me 109s attacking the capital. Taking to his parachute, he landed at Sarre near Canterbury and was taken prisoner. He later stated that the Luftwaffe were beginning to feel the effects of being constantly mauled by the RAF. Instead of the promised reduction in fighter opposition over England promised by Goering and his commanders, there were more spirited attacks then ever by the Hurricanes and Spitfires of the RAF. He went on to say that, 'We in the front line were slowly but inexorably bleeding to death.'

And that is exactly what was happening. As the end of October approached, the enemy pilots gave of their best but it was not enough. Even at this late stage, Goering felt confident that Fighter Command was on its knees. He even allowed Mussolini, the Italian dictator, to persuade him to send an armada of the Regia Aeronautica, the Italian air force, to participate in what he considered were to be the last raids on England before the invasion took place. As this unfamiliar sight crossed Kent, the ack-ack gunners opened fire, with the result that the large formation turned and headed for home without dropping a single bomb. Only when they crossed Ramsgate did several bombs fall into open fields. The only possible success they could claim was the propaganda for the Italian press!

In harbours along the French coast, October saw the barges and boats intended for the invasion of England slowly disappear. *Operation Sealion* was dead. German losses in October were large. A total of 325 Luftwaffe aircraft were lost, together with most of their crews, whilst Fighter Command losses in terms of pilots were 110 killed and 85 wounded.

By the beginning of November the battle was over. It petered out as the Luftwaffe withdrew entirely from the daylight raids and winter set in. During November, Goering issued new orders for attacks on Britain. The entire weight of the Luftwaffe would be concentrated on bombing major cities, industry and ports by night. Already during October, London had received more then 7,000 tons of bombs, with all the major cities receiving a less but equally devastating amount.

'Sailor' Malan who commanded No 74 Squadron at Biggin Hill in October 1940. (IWM)

Veterans of the Battle – No 72 Squadron complete with mascot at Biggin Hill in 1941.
(Fox Photos)

Many of the country's airfields, and those in Kent in particular, had virtually reached a state of becoming non-operational, so heavy had been the enemy attacks. But for the change in German policy, a few more weeks of bombing of such intensity might have brought a different outcome to the battle. The tactics used by Dowding, Park, and all the other commanders during that long, hot summer had worked.

At the end of the battle, however, Dowding and Park received very little recognition and were removed from their positions to take up mediocre duties. Sometime later a controversy arose in military circles as to their treatment. It was suggested by Sir Archibald Sinclair, the Secretary of State for Air, and Sir Trafford Leigh-Mallory, the Commander of 12 Group, that if the 'big wing' theory put forward by them in 1940 had been implemented immediately, much greater losses would have been inflicted on the Luftwaffe. This argument carries on to this day. There are also those who support entirely the tactics used by Dowding and Park. Whatever the answer, the Battle of Britain was won by the tactics of the time, by early warning radar and the Observer Corps, the ack-ack gunners on the ground, the army and the men and women of Fighter Command.

Air Vice Marshal 'Stuffy' Dowding, Commander-in-Chief, Fighter Command. (IWM)

A plaque dedicated to the people of Maidstone erected on the Maidstone Museum wall by local historian, Tony Webb. (Author)

We must also not forget the civilian services that did stirling work in the face of great danger, together with the men and women who worked in factories and on the land. Winston Churchill summed up all of this when he spoke during the long, hot summer of 1940:

> This is a war of unknown warriors. The whole of the warring nations are involved, not only soldiers but the entire population, men, women and children. The fronts are everywhere. The trenches dug in towns and in the streets. Every village is fortified. Every road is barred. The front lines run through the factories. The workmen are soldiers with different weapons but the same courage.

The war was to rage for another five years. If the aerial battle in the skies above Kent and the neighbouring counties had been lost, we must assume that we would have entered a new and dark age. To Dowding's 'chicks', also known as 'the few', we forever owe a debt of gratitude.

FIGHTING FOR OUR LIVES

Shortly after the Battle of Britain ended, a Battle Fund was raised to buy aircraft by displaying them in towns. This fine shot shows a Vickers Wellington in the car park of a car dealer's showroom in Maidstone. (Kent Messenger -ref. 6833/19)

The superb RAF memorial at West Malling (Author)

THE SQUADRONS OF THE BATTLE OF BRITAIN

	Code	Name	Aircraft
No 1	JX	Cawnpore	Hurricane
No 3	QO		Hurricane
No 17	YB		Hurricane
No 19	QV		Spitfire
No 23	YP		Blenheim
No 25	ZK		Blenheim
No29	RO		Blenheim
No 32	GZ		Hurricane
No 41	EB		Spitfire
No 43	FT	China/British	Hurricane
No 46	PO	Uganda	Hurricane
No 54	KL		Spitfire
No 56	US	Punjab	Hurricane
No 64	SH		Spitfire
No 65	YT	East India	Spitfire
No 66	LZ		Spitfire
No 72	RN	Basutoland	Spitfire
No 73	TP		Hurricane
No 74	ZP		Spitfire
No 79	NV	Madras	Hurricane
No 85	VY		Hurricane
No 87	LK	United Province	Hurricane
No 92	QJ	East India	Spitfire
No 111	JU		Hurricane
No141	TW		Defiant
No 145	SO		Hurricane
No 151	DZ		Hurricane
No 152	SN	Hyderabad	Spitfire
No 213	AK	Ceylon	Spitfire

No 219	FK	Mysore	Blenheim
No 222	ZD	Natal	Spitfire
No 229	KE		Hurricane
No 232	EF		Hurricane
No 234	AZ	Madras	Spitfire
No 238	VK		Hurricane
No 242	LE	Canadian	Hurricane
No 245	DX	Rhodesia	Hurricane
No 247	HP	China-British	Gladiator
No 249	GN	Gold Coast	Hurricane
No 253	SW	Hyderabad	Hurricane
No 257	DT	Burma	Hurricane
No 263	HE	Fellowship of the Bellows	Hurricane/Whirlwind
No 264	PS	Madras	Defiant
No 266	UO	Rhodesia	Spitfire
FLIGHTS			
No 421	LZ		Hurricane/Spitfire
No 422			Hurricane
Fighter Interception Unit	ZQ		Hurricane/Blenheim/ Beaufighter
AUXILIARY SQUADRONS			
No 501	SD	County of Gloucester	Hurricane
No 504	TM	County of Nottinghamshire	Hurricane
No 600	BQ	City of London	Blenheim/Beaufighter
No 601	UF	County of London	Hurricane
No 602	LO	City of Glasgow	Spitfire
No 603	XT	City of Edinburgh	Spitfire
No 604	NG	County of Middlesex	Spitfire
No 605	UP	County of Warwick	Hurricane
No 607	AF	County of Durham	Hurricane

No 609	PR	West Riding	Spitfire
No 610	DW	County of Chester	Spitfire
No 611	FY	West Lancashire	Spitfire
No 615	KW	County of Surrey	Hurricane
No 616	YQ	South Yorkshire	Spitfire
COMMONWEALTH AND ALLIED SQUADRONS			
No 1 Canadian	YO		Hurricane
No 302 (Polish)	WX	City of Poznan	Hurricane
No 303 (Polish)	RF	Warsaw/Kosciuszko	Hurricane
No 310 (Czech)	NN	Czecho Slovak	Hurricane
No 312 (Czech)	DU	Czecho-Slovak	Hurricane
COASTAL COMMAND			
No 235	QY		Blenheim
No 236	FA		Blenheim
No 248	WR		Blenheim
FLEET AIR ARM			
No 804	K6		Sea Gladiator/Martlet
No 808			Fulmer

BIBLIOGRAPHY

Battle of Britain: Then and Now, After the Battle, 1980

Bekker, Cajus, *The Luftwaffe War Diaries,* Corgi, 1969

Boorman, H.R.P, *Hell's Corner 1940: Kent becomes the Battlefield of Britain,* Kent Messenger, Maidstone, 1940

Brooks, Robin J., *Kent's Own 500 Squadron*, Meresborough, 1980

Burt, Kendal & Leasor, James, *The One that Got Away,* Pen & Sword Military Classics, 2006

Chant, Chris, *Aircraft of WW2,* Alder Books, 1999

Collyer, D.G., *Shellfire Memories Vols 1 & 2*, North Kent Books, 1992

Forrester, Larry, *Fly For Your Life*, Panther, 1959

Galland, Adolf, *The First and the Last,* Fontana, 1970

Halley, James J., *Squadrons of the RAF,* Air Britain, 1980

Hough, Richard & Richards, Denis, *The Battle of Britain Jubilee History,* Guild Publishing, 1990

Hyndman, Oonagh, *Wartime Kent,* Meresborough Books, 1990

Jefford, Wg Cdr C., *RAF Squadrons*, Airlife, 1988

Knight, Dennis, *Harvest of Messerschmitts*, Frederick Warne, 1981

Lyall, Gavin, *The War in the Air*, Hutchinson, 1968

Ogley, Bob, *Biggin on the Bump,* Froglet Publications, 1990

Philpott, Bryan, *German Fighters over England*, Patrick Stephens, 1979

Price, Alfred, *The Hardest Day,* 1986

Rootes, Andrew, *Front Line County*, Robert Hale, 1980

Steinhilper, Ulrich & Osborne, Peter, *Spitfire on my Tail*, Independent Books, 1990

Webb, Anthony, *Battle over Kent – Maidstone*

Wood, Derek & Dempster, Derek, *The Narrow Margin,* Hutchinson, 1961

INDEX